CW00460999

You can't fool God

You can't fool God

Peter Jeffery

EVANGELICAL PRESS

EVANGELICAL PRESS
Faverdale North Industrial Estate, Darlington, DL3 0PH,
England

Evangelical Press USA
P. O. Box 84, Auburn, MA 01501, USA

e-mail: sales@evangelicalpress.org

web: http://www.evangelicalpress.org

First published 2001

British Library Cataloguing in Publication Data available

ISBN 0 85234 488 0

Printed and bound in Great Britain by Creative Print & Design
Wales, Ebbw Vale

Contents

Introduction

One of the most terrible effects of sin in the human heart and mind is that it deludes us in just about every aspect of our understanding about God. The greatest delusion of all is to believe that there is no God, and that seems to be becoming a more popular opinion at the beginning of the twenty-first century.

But even those who say they believe in God may be subject to a delusion. We imagine we can reduce God to a size we can manipulate and control. One result of this is to think we can treat God in the same way as we treat each other. We can fool and deceive each other; so it follows that we can fool God. A 'God' whom we can deceive, and from whom we can hide things, is no God at all. The reality is that there is a God and that he cannot be fooled by us. He sees and knows all things. So what we consider to be secret sins are, as far as God is concerned, committed with blazing publicity.

Another delusion is that it is permissible to amend the laws of God, so that what the Bible considers to be sin is no longer regarded as sin by the modern mind. We modernize what God has said in order to soothe our consciences, but that does not change the fact that sin is still sin.

These delusions, and others, will one day be shown up for what they are and we shall have a rude awakening when God confronts us with our twisted beliefs and actions.

In this book we look at some biblical characters whose delusions ought to serve as a lesson to us all. Some were believers; others were not — but all had to face the consequences of their actions, either in this world or the next. Everyone who has some awareness of God, whether a keen believer or merely a nominal Christian, is capable of trying to fool him at some time or other and this book is written to remind us that this is an activity with no prospects of success.

1.

Believing a lie

Genesis 3

Delusions come in all shapes and sizes, but they always cause us to minimize something which is of great importance, or to exaggerate the significance of something that really is of little consequence. Modern man is guilty of the first of these with regard to the third chapter of Genesis. Everyone knows about Adam and Eve. If the details of the story are not clear, certainly the names are known. But the story is seen as an insignificant myth that has no bearing on the lives of men and women today.

The truth is that if Genesis 3 is not true then we do not need the rest of the Bible, because everything that follows is a consequence of the actions of Adam and Eve. In fact, if we do not understand what happened in Eden then we shall never understand the gospel. Man stopped listening to God, and this is as true now as ever it was. The consequences also are the same. If we don't listen to God we will listen to someone else. If we reject the truth of God we inevitably finish up believing a lie. That is what happened to Adam and Eve.

Eden

The Garden of Eden was made by God for Adam. This revealed something of the great love and concern God had for the man he had made in his own image. He wanted him to be happy and the garden contained everything necessary to achieve happiness and contentment, except one thing. Adam needed a 'helper suitable for him' (Genesis 2:18), and so God gave him Eve.

These two lived in perfect happiness in Eden so long as they lived God's way. Everything was there for them, but God made one law which they had to obey. It was not a harsh or unreasonable law. It in no way hindered their lifestyle, but it did remind them that God was their Lord and Creator and that he had a right to do as he thought best. The law was a demand for obedience and simply said, 'You are free to eat from any tree in the garden; but you must not eat from the tree of the knowledge of good and evil, for when you eat of it you will surely die' (Genesis 2:16-17).

Adam and Eve had no quarrel with this and continued to enjoy fellowship with God until they were faced with the lies of the devil. Then they rejected that one reasonable condition. Perhaps they thought the act of eating the fruit from the tree in the middle of the garden was not all that important. Perhaps they thought God would not mind if they disobeyed that one commandment. Whatever was in their minds, the fact was that they had stopped listening to God and the consequences were devastating.

Why did they do it?

Sin is excused today for all sorts of reasons, but Adam and Eve had no excuse whatsoever. They could not plead ignorance. They knew exactly what God had said and Eve could quote God's words to the devil. It is true that most people today are ignorant of what God says. We live in a world that knows little or nothing of the Bible, but it is a self-imposed ignorance. In countries like Britain and America Bibles are easily available and modern-language versions help people to understand what God says. Even in countries where the Bible is forbidden, there is what Romans 1:20 calls the clear revelation of 'God's invisible qualities'. This alone leaves men and women without an excuse for rejecting God.

Adam and Eve did not sin in some deprived slum where they struggled to maintain an existence. Their sin took place in paradise amidst the bounty of God's goodness to them.

They could not even plead that they were overwhelmed by the intensity of the devil's temptation. He did not apply strong pressure upon them; rather he simply asked a question: 'Did God really say, "You must not eat from any tree in the garden"?' Then the devil made a dogmatic assertion: 'You will not surely die.' The devil gave no reason for this but Adam and Eve accepted it. No proof was provided. The devil just contradicted the word of God and thus sowed a doubt in their minds.

Eventually all temptation comes down to this. Whether the temptation is sexual, financial, pride, or anything else,

the bottom line is: what does God say about it? If we have
no confidence in the Word of God, temptation does not
have to be intense for us to give in to it. For Eve the fact
that the fruit was 'good for food and pleasing to the eye'
was enough. But the fruit had always been like this and
she had never taken and eaten it before. The difference
now was that she believed the devil's lie. She was deceived. Adam, 'who was with her' during this time, followed his wife's example and he too ate the forbidden
fruit.

The New Testament says Adam was not deceived in
the same as way Eve was (1 Timothy 2:14). If he was not
deceived by the devil's lies, why did he sin? The passage
in 1 Timothy seems to suggest that he relinquished his
God-given responsibility for leadership and allowed his
wife to control the family decisions. If he simply followed a
bad example it meant that Adam cared very little for God's
commands. Yet again it comes back to the same thing —
God's Word is disregarded and the result is sin.

Good and evil

Genesis 2 ends with these words: 'The man and his wife
were both naked, and they felt no shame.' But no sooner
had sin become part of human nature than their nakedness disturbed them and they covered their bodies. Sin
opened their eyes to what they now were. In effect one
aspect of the devil's deceptive words was fulfilled, in that
they now knew both good and evil. In their sinless state

they had only known good. Their new knowledge was painful and they took steps to nullify it. Their answer was to sew fig leaves together.

Sin brings a sense of guilt, and men and women cannot bear the feeling of guilt, so every attempt is made to cover it up. What foolishness! Do we think that God is as easily deceived as we are? Once sin became part of Adam and Eve's experience there was a progression of actions that all sinners have followed ever since: firstly, cover it up; secondly, hide from God; and, thirdly, blame someone else for it.

Physical nakedness can be covered, but that was not really the problem; sin was. God makes this very clear in Genesis 3:11: 'Who told you that you were naked? Have you eaten from the tree from which I commanded you not to eat?' It was not their bodies but their souls that were first in rebellion against God. Their attempt to cover up was pathetic, but no more so than modern man's attempts to deal with his sin. Down through the centuries this has gone on, but now we have found the 'perfect' answer. In the thinking of men and women today there is no such thing as sin. The concept is regarded as dead, and there are no clear definitions of right or wrong. Everything is relative, so there are no absolute standards and the whole idea of sin is consigned to the scrap heap.

That reasoning could well provide the final solution to human sin and guilt, if only it were indeed in man's power to redefine the standards God has set. But God gives no regard to our rewriting of what is right and wrong. Sin still pays the same wages as it ever did — that is, death. And, for all our twisted logic, we ourselves cannot really find comfort in this concept and we still have to hide from God and run away from any divine reality.

Adam and Eve became afraid of the God they had previously loved and served. Sin caused the fear, and fear caused them to try to hide from God. It was a foolish action because no one can hide from Almighty God. Do we really think that God can be avoided? If we do not seek God, he still seeks us and asks us the same question that he put to Adam and Eve: 'Where are you?'

This question plagues our consciences. God still speaks through his Word, the Bible, and through the preaching of the gospel. That is why men and women will not read the Bible and ridicule preaching as boring and irrelevant. It is all part of our hiding from God. But God will not let us get away with it. He comes to us and confronts us with his truth. If he does not do so in this life, he certainly will do so at the Judgement Day when we must all stand before him.

What are we going to say when God confronts us? We shall no doubt seek to pass on the blame to someone else. Adam blamed Eve, and in so doing blamed God by referring to her as 'the woman you put with me'. Little has changed and God is still blamed for most of what is wrong in this world: 'Why does God allow all the evil in the world?' 'Why doesn't God do something about it?' But we cannot hope to get away with such evasion. We are responsible for our sin, not God.

Eve blamed the serpent. 'It's the devil's fault,' she said. 'It wasn't me, but evil influences acting against me!' How often do we excuse our sin with some variation of Eve's plea? But we can't fool God. All sin is a rejection of God's authority and there is no excuse for it. No sin is excusable, but, thank God, in the gospel of Jesus Christ all sin can be pardoned.

Questions for personal thought or group discussion

1. Is Genesis 3 really the key to understanding the message of the Bible?
2. Why did God issue the command concerning the tree in the middle of the garden?
3. What do you consider to be the believer's main defence against temptation?
4. Is a sense of guilt something to be avoided?

2.

'It wasn't my fault'

Exodus 32; Deuteronomy 9:7-29

It is not clever to sin. Sin is a denial of the greatest fact about man — namely, that he is made in the image of God. Sin always makes a person less of a man or woman. In fact, just about the most foolish thing anyone can do is to sin. Yet we find it so easy and so enjoyable that it appears to be the most natural thing to do. This appearance is a delusion and our own behaviour when we sin reveals how ridiculous it is. Aaron, the brother of Moses, is a classic example of this.

A good man

Aaron was a good man and had played a crucial part in the exodus of God's people from Egypt. He had acted as Moses' spokesman before Pharaoh and Moses was later to consecrate him as the first high priest. In this capacity Aaron alone was allowed into the Holy of Holies once a year on the Day of Atonement as the representative of the people. So when Moses went up Mount Sinai to meet with God he probably thought he was leaving the people in good hands under the leadership of Aaron.

Subsequent events proved that, although Aaron was a good man he was also a weak one who was unable to cope with the pressures of leadership. More than that, he was a foolish man who, when confronted with his sin, came out with the most ridiculous of excuses, pleading that what he did was not his fault.

A weak leader

Moses had been away for forty days and the people were growing restless. They did not know how to wait and felt lost without someone to tell them what to do. They do not seem to have had much respect for Moses, for they referred to him as 'this fellow Moses' (Exodus 32:1). They did not know what had happened to him and did not appear to care. So they asked Aaron to 'Make us gods who will go before us.' These people were characterized by an incredible spiritual blindness. They knew from very recent experience that the Lord God was not a man-made god, but the eternal living God who had demonstrated his love and power on their behalf. The Egyptian gods were home-made and totally useless. They had seen this, and no one could doubt what had recently taken place; yet they wanted a man-made god to lead them.

Aaron should have done what Stephen was to do centuries later and forcefully reminded them of who the Lord is and what he had done for them (Acts 7). Instead he crumbled under the pressure of popular opinion and made a golden calf for the Israelites to worship (Exodus 32:2-4). To be fair to Aaron, popular opinion is never an easy foe to oppose. But he does not appear to have raised any objections, or even to have pleaded with Israel to wait for Moses to return. Instead of opposing their request, he made them a new god with his own hands. Leaders like this have been a blight on the people of God ever since. Bishops and preachers who are afraid to give a lead are more deadly than atheists who pour scorn on the Christian faith. Leaders are meant to lead, not follow, and in this Aaron failed miserably.

Aaron then attempted to give his sin a veneer of religious respectability by building an altar in front of the calf and announcing that the next day would be a festival to the Lord. Had this man no concept of the reality and awesomeness of the Lord he was supposed to be serving? And are we today so foolish as to think that we can reject the Jesus Christ of the New Testament and replace him with a superstar who has no power and no authority? Is God to be mocked in this way?

Leadership of the people of God has never been an easy task. The only way to survive is with the Lord's help. Moses made mistakes but he was always concerned to please God, not the people, and he therefore knew the reality of God's presence with him. Aaron feared the people more than he did God and he allowed them to lead him. To be a good man is not enough in spiritual leadership. The leader must, above all things, be aware that God has put him into the position of leadership which he occupies and his top priority must be to please God.

The Jewish leaders in Acts 5 placed Peter and the apostles in a similar situation to Aaron. Their demand was that Jesus was to be ignored and the gospel message silenced. Peter's response still stands as an unalterable standard for Christian leaders: 'We must obey God rather than men!' (Acts 5:29). This made the Jews furious and the lives of the apostles were put in danger as a result. No doubt Aaron would have faced a similar reaction if he had refused to make the people a god. The difference between the apostles and Aaron was that, while the former 'left the Sanhedrin, rejoicing because they had been counted worthy of suffering disgrace for the Name' (Acts 5:41), Aaron was not even prepared to voice an objection against godlessness. The result was that, while the apostles experienced great blessing from God, Aaron was to witness the judgement of God. Three thousand Jews died under God's wrath and his own life was only spared because of a special plea by Moses on his behalf (Deuteronomy 9:20).

Moses confronts Aaron

Moses' initial response to the sin and idolatry of Israel was one of intercession as he pleaded with God to spare them (Exodus 32:11-14), but that did not curb his own anger against them. When he actually saw the calf and the way the people were behaving before it, he was so furious that he smashed the two stone tablets on which the Ten Commandments were recorded. Israel had broken the law of God and by his action Moses demonstrated that they were no longer worthy to receive this special revelation of God. Then Moses dealt with the golden calf. He completely destroyed it, 'ground it to powder, scattered it on the water and made the Israelites drink it' (Exodus 32:20).

He then confronted Aaron with the question: 'What did these people do to you, that you led them into such great sin?' Moses imagined that the people must have exerted great pressure upon his brother for Aaron to have acted as he had. Sadly, it had not needed great pressure to persuade Aaron to make the idol. A weak man bends easily when faced with public opinion.

It is clear that Moses blamed Aaron for what had happened, but his brother was not prepared to accept the blame. He first of all accused the people — and to an extent they were to blame — but then he went on to make what must be one of the most pathetic excuses for sin ever recorded in the Scriptures: 'Then they gave me the gold, and I threw it into the fire, and out came this calf!' (Exodus 32:24). He was in effect saying, 'It wasn't my fault. All I did was to throw the gold into the fire and out popped the calf.' Moses did not dignify such an excuse with an answer.

The excuse was a lie, as we can see from verse 4, because Aaron had, in fact, '[fashioned] it with a tool'. That was bad enough, but the sheer stupidity of the excuse is amazing. Did Aaron really think anyone would believe that? Did he think that God would accept such nonsense? Or was it another instance of this weak man collapsing under pressure and speaking without thinking? Sin can do this to us. It warps our reason and distorts our thinking.

How often have we tried to explain away our sin with similar twisted reasoning? 'It wasn't my fault,' is paraded

daily by sinners before God, accompanied by the most
ridiculous adornments that would not fool a ten-year-old,
let alone Almighty God. Let us remember that Aaron was
not a godless heathen, but a man who had experienced
the blessings of God. What we have here is the equivalent
of what happens when a Christian refuses to accept the
responsibility for his sin and invents nonsense to explain
it.

We have to realize that our sin is always our fault. Christ
took the responsibility for that sin and faced the punishment it deserved when he died on the cross, but we were
the ones who committed the sin and it is therefore our
fault. The only way for a Christian to act when he or she is
guilty of sin is to repent. Excuses and explanations are of
no use. They merely serve to show that we are not fully
accepting the blame. However, 'If we confess our sin, he is
faithful and just and will forgive us our sin, and purify us
from all unrighteousness' (1 John 1:9).

Questions for personal thought or group discussion

1. How is it possible to be a good man and yet a weak one
at the same time?
2. Should popular opinion have a major influence upon
our thinking?
3. What do you make of Aaron's excuse in Exodus 32:24?
4. Is there ever any excuse for sin?

3.

The writing is on the wall

Daniel 5

Belshazzar was King of Babylon in succession to the famous King Nebuchadnezzar. One day he gave a great banquet and invited 1,000 guests. In the middle of the festivities, when everyone was drinking heavily, he decided to bring in the golden goblets that Nebuchadnezzar had taken from the temple in Jerusalem. These goblets had been dedicated to the worship of the Lord, and Belshazzar no doubt thought it was a great joke to use them to praise idols. So what we have here is a man quite deliberately scorning and mocking the Lord God.

There was a time when most unbelievers had some respect for religion. Jokes about God were taboo — but not any longer. At the beginning of the twenty-first century the attitude displayed by Belshazzar is rampant again. Nothing is sacred today, and this is not only true of men in a drunken stupor. We see it in TV programmes, where so often it seems that the actors go out of their way to scorn the things of God. We could well ask, 'Why doesn't God do something about it? Why does he put up with it?'

The answer is to be found in the story of two neighbouring farmers. One was a Christian who, apart from tending to the animals, would not work his farm on Sundays. The other was a very worldly man who often made fun of his neighbour's religious convictions. One year he told his Christian friend of a scheme he had concocted. He was going to plant and care for one of his fields only on Sundays. He would not touch it during the week. Everything that needed doing was to be done on a Sunday. His challenge to his Christian friend was: 'Let's see if your God punishes me with a bad harvest.'

Harvest came and the unbeliever was delighted when his 'Sunday only' field yielded a much better crop than usual. He taunted the Christian with this fact and demanded to know why God hadn't stopped him. The Christian farmer took all the abuse quietly and then said, 'God does not call in all his accounts at once, but he will call them in.'

No one can scorn and challenge God and get away with it. God does, and will do, something. Belshazzar did not get away with mocking God, and nor will we!

The fingers

In the middle of the king's drunken revelry a most remarkable thing happened: 'Suddenly the fingers of a human hand appeared and wrote on the plaster on the wall.' Belshazzar never sobered up so quickly in his life. He was terrified. All the colour drained from his face and his knees knocked in fear. His laughing and mocking had stopped.

Something was happening that he could not understand but that he could not ignore.

He sent for his advisers, but they were all baffled. Eventually he summoned Daniel to the royal presence and only then was the meaning of the writing on the wall made clear to him.

God can very quickly change a situation. He does not need our permission to intervene in man's affairs. We may think that God is a joke and that we can live our lives without him. Belshazzar at his party thought that, but the writing was on the wall for this man and that very night he died. God is not to be played around with. He will not be mocked, and it is time we took God seriously.

The expression, 'The writing is on the wall', has become part of the English language to mean that there are clear signs of trouble ahead. Throughout the Bible the finger of God writes for us the inevitable consequences of sin.

- 'The wages of sin is death' (Romans 6:23).
- 'Be sure that your sin will find you out' (Numbers 32:23).
- 'Sin, when it is full-grown, gives birth to death' (James 1:15).

It should therefore come as no surprise to us when God deals with sin, and yet men and women are always surprised by divine judgement. When eventually they are confronted with God, their reaction will be exactly like that of Belshazzar.

Daniel's interpretation

When the prophet Daniel was brought in he began to deal with the situation, not by interpreting the writing, but by showing Belshazzar why this was happening to him: 'But you ... O Belshazzar, have not humbled yourself, though you knew all this. Instead, you have set yourself up against the Lord of heaven. You had the goblets from his temple brought to you, and you and your nobles, your wives and your concubines drank wine from them. You praised the gods of silver and gold, of bronze, iron, wood and stone, which cannot see or hear or understand. But you did not honour the God who holds in his hand your life and all your ways. Therefore he sent the hand that wrote the inscription' (Daniel 5:22-24).

Belshazzar knew something that should have prevented him from sinking to the situation of scorning God. He had access to information that could have prevented him from incurring the judgement of God in this way. The reason why this was about to happen to him was not the fact that he was a drunkard and a thoroughly corrupt man, but that he had rejected the light that God had shone into his life. The words of Daniel to the king, 'though you knew all this', are the crux of God's condemnation of him.

Nothing much has changed over the years and Jesus said of the people of his day, 'This is the verdict: Light has come into the world, but men loved darkness instead of light because their deeds were evil' (John 3:19). There is grace enough in Christ to forgive any amount of sin, but when men reject the light that God shines into their hearts, when they reject the gospel, there is nothing left but judgement and hell.

What did Belshazzar know?

The knowledge that Belshazzar had, but which he did not act upon, is recorded for us in Daniel 5:18-21. It concerned God's dealings with his predecessor, Nebuchadnezzar. Belshazzar should have learnt from the life of Nebuchadnezzar, and if he had done so, and had humbled himself before God, there would have been no writing on the wall for him.

Nebuchadnezzar was a pagan king with no knowledge of God; yet God knew him and was at work in his life: 'The Most High God gave your father Nebuchadnezzar sovereignty and greatness and glory and splendour...' (5:18).

Let us see how God began to reveal himself to this pagan king in the first four chapters of Daniel's book.

Daniel 1

Nebuchadnezzar was, for the first time in his life, brought into contact with men who lived in obedience to the living God. He was greatly impressed with what he saw because their faith was so unlike the formal religion of Babylon. He had seen nothing like this before. Here were young men for whom God was so real that they were willing to forsake a life of ease in order to be faithful to him. For the first time he was made aware of the true God.

Daniel 2

Nebuchadnezzar had ignored the truth God had placed before him, but God continued to deal with him and sent him bad dreams. This brought him once again into contact with Daniel, who interpreted the dreams for the king. He was led to confess, 'Surely your God is the God of gods and the Lord of kings!' (v. 27).

Daniel 3

In spite of his acknowledgement of the supremacy of God, the king built a huge idol. He had experienced the mercies and blessings of God, and had acknowledged that there is no God like him, but he refused to submit and returned to his old ways. He had, in New Testament language, become hardened against the gospel and he could no longer tolerate the faithfulness of Shadrach, Meshach and Abednego, which he had so admired in chapter 1.

It is amazing that God continued to be patient with this man, but he did, and demonstrated once more his power in the incident of the fiery furnace. Once again Nebuchadnezzar acknowledged the greatness of God: 'No other god can save in this way' (v. 29). This was encouraging, but it fell far short of a personal faith.

Daniel 4

Nebuchadnezzar was still running away from God, so the Lord sent him more bad dreams. The king had no peace or contentment and God would not leave him alone. Daniel interpreted the dream, as he had done on previous occasions, but the message he had for Nebuchadnezzar was not a pleasant one: 'This is the interpretation, O king, and this is the decree the Most High has issued against my lord the king: You will be driven away from people and will live with the wild animals ... your kingdom will be restored to you when you acknowledge that Heaven rules. Therefore, O king, be pleased to accept my advice: Renounce your sins by doing what is right, and your wickedness by being kind to the oppressed. It may be that then your prosperity will continue' (vv. 24-27).

How did the king respond to this warning? He knew that Daniel had been right before, so this should have given him a sense of urgency to obey the word of God. But for a whole year he did nothing. Perhaps after a while he convinced himself that Daniel had got it wrong. He even began to be self-confident again: 'He said, "Is not this the great Babylon I have built as the royal residence, by my mighty power and for the glory of my majesty?"' (v. 30).

The words were hardly out of his mouth when God's judgement fell on him and all that Daniel had said came true. People say that if you take religion too seriously you will go mad. Here is the proof that this is a lie. Nebuchadnezzar went mad because he ignored God. God is not fooled by men's words, but he is amazingly patient, and eventually the king's madness passed and he came to true spiritual health and salvation.

'Though you knew all this'

This is what Belshazzar had seen and known, but he had learnt nothing from it. On the contrary, he scorned and abused the God who had so evidently been active in the life of Nebuchadnezzar.

Many people are like this. They vigorously reject every evidence of the reality of God that is put before them. They sin, not in ignorance, but quite deliberately. Light has come to them, but they have chosen evil and darkness instead. Like Belshazzar, '[they do] not honour the God who holds in his hand [their] life and all [their] ways'. If we will not have the mercy of God, then inevitably we are left with the wrath of God.

Belshazzar demanded to know what the writing on the wall meant. Daniel told him:

> *Mene:* God has numbered the days of your reign and brought it to an end.
> *Tekel:* You have been weighed on the scales and found wanting.
> *Peres:* Your kingdom is divided and given to the Medes and Persians.

Unlike Nebuchadnezzar, Belshazzar did not have twelve months to think about it, and he died that same night.

God is amazingly patient with us but even his patience will come to an end. We are all weighed in the scales and found wanting. We are all sinners and therefore unacceptable to God. The writing is on the wall for all of us. There is only one hope: 'When you were dead in your sins and in the uncircumcision of your sinful nature, God made you alive with Christ. He forgave us all our sins, having cancelled the written code, with its regulations, that was against us and that stood opposed to us; he took it away, nailing it to the cross' (Colossians 2:13-14).

Our only hope is the cross of Jesus Christ because there Jesus dealt with our sin and rebellion, our stubbornness and rejection of God. There we can find salvation and peace with God.

Questions for personal thought or group discussion

1. How do men and women today show their scorn for God?

2. Why do you think God chose 'the writing on the wall' to deal with Belshazzar?

3. Does modern man have access to information that could prevent him from foolishly mocking God?

4. What is the main lesson we can learn from the story of Belshazzar?

4.

Whitewash

Ezekiel 13

Whitewash is a cheap and easy way to cover up a poor job. It covers over the cracks and blemishes, and to a casual glance it can make a flimsy wall look as if it is in a reasonable state. Using whitewash in this way is dishonest and deceitful, but it will fool many people. However, such actions never fool God. In Ezekiel 13 the prophet speaks of people who build a shoddy wall and then cover it with whitewash. God's response is: 'Tell those who cover it with whitewash that it is going to fall.'

False prophets

Ezekiel 13 shows what a high value God places on the truth and how strongly he opposes those who deny and distort it. He calls them false prophets and says, 'I am against you' (v. 8). Such men have always troubled the people of God. Ezekiel clearly had to deal with them and in the New Testament Paul was battling against the same problem all the time. False prophets are still with us. We are living in days when people believe that there is no such thing as absolute truth about God — only opinions. In such a climate false prophets thrive.

The mark of the false prophet is that he ignores the claims of Jesus, scorns the Bible and presents his own ideas as if they were the truth of God. God says of such men that they 'prophesy out of their own imagination' (v. 2). These people may appear charming, delightful, pleasant, and may even sincerely believe that what they say is true, but God is against them because the damage they do is horrific.

In verse 22 God tells us that false prophets do two deadly things: they dishearten true believers and they encourage the wicked. True believers are disheartened as they have to face attacks upon the truth of Scripture, and very often also upon their own conversion experience. As if that was not bad enough, these false prophets actually encourage the wicked. When it is preached that because God is love all are going to heaven, irrespective of their beliefs or actions, then sinners are led to believe there is no need for them to repent.

These people in fact teach lies which encourage unbelief. If all paths lead to God then the uniqueness of Jesus Christ as the only Saviour is denied. If ministers at funeral services pronounce over everyone, indiscriminately, that the deceased is being buried 'in sure and certain hope of resurrection from the dead', then the impression given is that ultimately it does not matter what he or she believed. But it does matter. The problem is so serious that

Jesus warned of wolves in sheep's clothing. The ones who wear sheep's clothing are normally shepherds, so Jesus is warning of wolves pretending to be shepherds, of false prophets leading his people astray.

False Christianity

The heart of false Christianity is that it does not take God seriously, and consequently it does not take sin seriously. It is impossible to take sin seriously if God is ignored, and there can be no true Christianity without an awareness of the holiness of God and his attitude to sin.

The false prophet preaches an easy-believism. He promises peace with God but denies the only way in which such peace can be obtained. As a result people are led astray. God equates this false promise of peace, when in fact there is no peace, with whitewashing a flimsy wall. All through Scripture God makes it clear that he will not tolerate sin. The false prophet breeds a false Christianity that refuses to take God seriously on the question of sin. People are thus lulled into a false sense of security.

An old lady in her seventies who had all her life been a member of a church where the gospel was never preached, by the grace of God heard the gospel for the first time. She realized that she was not a Christian and conviction of sin made her believe she needed to be saved. So she went to talk to her minister about it. He told her she was being silly. She was a good person, he said, and only evil people like prostitutes and drug addicts needed to be saved.

He talked her out of conviction of sin. The following week this old lady died suddenly.

Thousands today are being deceived by statements such as, 'The God I believe in is a God of love,' which may sound reasonable enough. However, very often the declaration of the truth of God's love carries with it the implication that there is no such thing as divine anger, no judgement, no punishment for sin, and therefore no hell. It may sound very attractive, but it is a deadly lie. It is peace, peace, when there is no peace.

It is this sort of wrong teaching that inevitably encourages the use of whitewash.

A cover-up

False prophets always bypass the question of human sin and guilt, and in so doing they are guilty of a cover-up. God, in speaking to Ezekiel, uses the picture of people building a wall — probably the city walls which were meant to protect against an enemy. They build a flimsy wall — one that is easy and quick to erect, made from shoddy materials. They know their work is of poor quality, so to cover up the deficiency they give the wall a coat of whitewash. This makes it look attractive but it is still useless as a defence, and God says it will fall.

The application of this can be seen everywhere today. People are encouraged to build flimsy walls of their own self-righteousness. Easygoing religion delights in sentimental doctrine that insists there must always be a feeling of well-being. Nothing must be allowed to disturb the spiritual and moral sleep of its hearers. So we must not mention sin, and certainly never preach repentance. People love this and they come to think of church as some sort of emotional aspirin to make them feel good. But it is all whitewash. It is a refusal to face the reality of the situation, which is that the way men and women are building their lives is flimsy and unacceptable to Almighty God.

Some years ago, just before a general election, one of the candidates turned up in our church. In a conversation with him after the service, he told me how busy he was as a politician and that consequently he did not attend church very often. He said that when he had time he liked to go to the old parish church, where he found the stillness, stained glass windows and organ music so relaxing. I told him that that was not Christianity but escapism. Reluctantly he had to agree with me. But how many folk are like this? Their Christianity bears no resemblance to the faith of the New Testament.

We whitewash our lives by trusting our own goodness and efforts. We then compare ourselves with others and conclude that we are better than they are, so everything must be all right. Such belief is possible by making our Christianity man-centred instead of God-centred. What God thinks is not considered at all. This makes it easy then to reject the gospel call for repentance and the need to seek Jesus for pardon and mercy. How many men and women there are who outwardly appear upright and respectable, kind and gracious in their relations with others, but it is all a cover-up and their hearts remain unchanged.

Jesus likened such people to whitewashed tombs — clean and white on the outside but full of death inside (see Matthew 23:27).

Whitewash is easy to apply, but the trouble is that it does not last. It wears off and when the rain comes in torrents it washes away and the job has to be done all over again.

God's answer

When I was a boy I lived in a very old house that could only be called a slum. It was during the years of the Second World War and very few new houses were being built. Our house had two rooms upstairs and two down, but we could only use one of the bedrooms and one room downstairs because of damp and decay. The backyard was about ten foot (3 meters) square. It had a high wall all around and the toilet was in the far corner from the house. We had to use the yard continually because the toilet was out there, but it was in a dreadful mess. The walls, like the house itself, were crumbling and decaying. To keep the yard looking reasonably tidy my father would whitewash the walls every year. When the job was first done the walls looked lovely and sparkling, but we knew the whitewash only covered up the decaying brickwork underneath. This went on for years until after the war the local council condemned the house as unfit to live in and moved us out into a new one. After that there was no longer any need for whitewash.

Isn't that like many lives? They are spiritually decaying and God condemns them. They may be morally impeccable but spiritually they are a slum. God is not fooled by whatever veneer we cover ourselves with, and it is all so unnecessary because the God who condemns our sin is willing to move us out and provide a new life for us in the Lord Jesus Christ.

Questions for personal thought or group discussion

1. Why does God speak so strongly against false prophets?
2. If many false prophets are charming, delightful and even sincere, how are we to react to them?
3. Do you think there is any whitewash in your life?

5.

You can wash your hands but the guilt remains

Luke 23:1-25; Matthew 27:11-26

Most of us protest our innocence passionately when accused of some wrongdoing. Sometimes the protest is justified because we are wrongly accused, but at other times it is just a smokescreen, or a refusal on our part to face up to the facts. We may even succeed in convincing ourselves of our innocence because we cannot cope with the shame of being guilty of some particular wrong action. Whatever the rights or wrongs of the case, most of us are good at protesting our innocence.

Have you ever seen a rugby international on TV and watched the face of a front-row forward when penalized by the referee for some violation of the rules? With wide-eyed innocence he looks in amazement at the referee. His expression seems to say, 'How could you possibly think I would do such a thing?'

Often we can fool other people by our protests of innocence, but no one fools God. We may even make a dramatic demonstration in support of our claims, like Pontius Pilate's action when he washed his hands and declared, 'I am innocent of this man's blood' (Matthew 27:24), but

God knows the true state of the case. Pilate may well have believed he was innocent, but God's verdict was different and he held Pilate accountable (Acts 4:27).

Pilate

Pontius Pilate was the Roman procurator of Judea and Samaria. He hated the Jews and they in turn hated him. He was not a very tactful man and once allowed Roman soldiers to enter the holy city of Jerusalem with ensigns bearing the image of the emperor. To a Jew this was sacrilege and no governor had allowed it before. On another occasion he used money from the temple treasury to pay for an aqueduct. This caused a riot in which many Jews were killed. It is probably this incident that is referred to in Luke 13:1, where we read of 'the Galileans whose blood Pilate had mixed with their sacrifices'.

The Jews had cause to hate Pilate, but in order to kill Jesus they needed him because he alone had the power to pronounce the death sentence on Jesus which they so desperately wanted. So they woke Pilate up in the middle of the night and brought the Lord Jesus before him. He would certainly have heard about Jesus. Everyone in Jerusalem must have heard about the Galilean, but now Jesus was there in front of him and he had to make a decision.

Pilate was no fool and he immediately realized that Jesus had been brought before him on a trumped-up charge. He said, 'I find no basis for a charge against this man' (Luke 23:4). He wanted to release Jesus but did not do so. Pilate was under pressure. His past foolishness had caused the Jews to riot. On the last occasion this had earned him a severe rebuke from Caesar, so he could not afford more trouble. Self-interest, coupled with a weak moral character, caused him to look for a convenient way out of his dilemma.

The answer seemed to be to send Jesus to Herod. Jesus was from Galilee and therefore under Herod's jurisdiction, so he decided to let the king deal with the problem. But this did not work and Herod sent Jesus back.

While Pilate was dithering and looking for a way out, a remarkable thing happened: 'His wife sent him this message: "Don't have anything to do with that innocent man, for I have suffered a great deal today in a dream because of him"' (Matthew 27:19). Why should this woman dream about Jesus? There seems to be no explanation other than that God was warning Pontius Pilate through his wife that Jesus did not deserve a death sentence. To pronounce the verdict the Jews wanted would clearly be a miscarriage of justice. Pilate knew what the right thing to do was, but he wanted someone else to take the decision. So the choice of Barabbas or Christ was put before the crowd. At that point, with the priests and elders urging them on, they would have chosen the devil himself rather than Christ. But Pilate was satisfied. As he saw things, it was not now his responsibility but that of the Jews.

Hand-washing

When Pilate washed his hands to declare his innocence he was trying to impress, not God, but the Jewish crowd, so he chose a Jewish ritual in order to do so. In Deuteronomy 21:6-7 we read, 'Then all the elders of the town nearest the body shall wash their hands over the heifer whose neck was broken in the valley, and they shall declare: "Our hands did not shed this blood, nor did our eyes see it done." ' Here is another biblical phrase that has become part of the English language. 'To wash one's hands of something' means today exactly what it did for Pilate. He was having nothing more to do with the trial of Jesus and declaring that whatever happened afterwards was not his responsibility.

The action went down well with the crowd and they were quite willing to accept the responsibility: 'Let his blood be on us and on our children!' (Matthew 27:25). God was not so easily appeased and in his eyes Pilate was as guilty as the crowd.

Sin cannot be atoned for by religious ritual or pleas of innocence; yet we all try it. And even if our consciences are satisfied by the thought that we tried our best, God is not satisfied with this. We can silence our consciences, but we cannot fool God. It is not difficult to see how wrong Pilate was in denying any responsibility for the death of Jesus. True, he saw he was getting nowhere with the trial, but that was because he refused to exercise the authority he had as Roman governor. He had control of the soldiers and one word from him would have sent the crowd away to their homes. But he would not use the power he had. He had the warning from the person who loved him most, but he ignored that. Therefore washing his hands did not remove the guilt. Spurgeon once said, 'Pilate, you need something stronger than water to wash the blood of that just person off your hands. You cannot rid yourself of responsibility by that farce. He who has power to prevent a wrong is guilty of the act if he permits others to do it, even though he does not actually commit it himself.'[1]

Our problem is seeing how easily we can go down the same road as Pilate. It is possible to acknowledge the goodness of Jesus, to say he was a great man, and yet to deny all he said about being the incarnate God. A man says, 'I think very highly of Jesus', and yet at the same time ignores the fact that Jesus said we cannot be Christians unless we are born again. We admire Jesus but dismiss his absolute statements as nothing more than a matter of opinion. If someone was to tell us that we were not Christians at all we might well be offended, but if the same person said we were not born again, it would not bother us. Yet, according to Jesus, there is no such thing as a Christian who is not born again. We say we respect Jesus, but wash our hands of all his essential teaching on the way of salvation.

Clearly Pilate wanted to be innocent of the death of Jesus, but wanting is as useless as washing. He could have pleaded that the cross was all part of God's plan and that he was merely an instrument in making it possible. He could even have quoted Scripture to defend his position, but God is not fooled.

The fact is that God holds us all responsible for our own sin. Circumstances, temptation, bad company and a whole host of things affect us all. But they do not cancel out our responsibility. 'Guilty' is stamped on all our hearts and there is only one thing that can remove it. Pilate made reference to 'this man's blood', and the New Testament delights to tell us that salvation from sin and guilt is found only in the shed blood of the atoning death of Jesus on the cross: 'For you know that it was not with perishable things such as silver or gold that you were redeemed from the empty way of life handed down to you from your fore-fathers, but with the precious blood of Christ, a lamb with-out blemish or defect' (1 Peter 1:18-19).

If we ignore what God says about the death of his Son then it will not matter what else we do; it will all be as useless as washing our hands and pleading innocence.

Questions for personal thought or group discussion

1. Why are we so quick to protest our innocence?
2. What do you think of the dream Pilate's wife had?
3. Discuss what Spurgeon said about Pilate.
4. Why was Pilate so anxious to be innocent of the death of Jesus?

6.

The kiss of a friend

John 13:18-30; Matthew 26:47-56

Normally the kiss of a friend is something pleasant to receive. It is an indication of love and affection and most
folk enjoy being kissed. Judas Iscariot gave the kiss another dimension when he used it to betray Jesus. A Judas-
kiss is something no one wants. It spells treachery and
betrayal.

Judas was a strange character. He appears to have been
the odd one out among the twelve apostles. His name
indicates that he came from Judea, while the other eleven
were Galileans. Did this cause resentment, as he perhaps
felt an outsider? If so, there would have been no justifi-
cation for this, for he was given the only 'official' position
among the apostles, namely that of treasurer (John 12:6).
In the passage where we learn of this John makes some
devastating comments about Judas. He says he had no
concern for the poor. In other words, he was totally at
variance with the heart and mind of Christ, who continually showed compassion to the poor. Judas was like a hired
hand who 'when he sees the wolf coming … abandons

the sheep and runs away… The man runs away because he is a hired hand and cares nothing for the sheep' (John 10:12-13).

That in itself would have been bad enough for someone who was an apostle, but John goes on to say that Judas was a thief who helped himself to the money in the common purse. John probably made this comment with hindsight and it is unlikely that any of the other apostles were aware of Judas' true character before the betrayal, but Jesus knew.

The motive of betrayal

Some have tried to defend Judas by arguing that he really was a true servant of Christ but grew impatient with the speed at which things were happening. The betrayal, they claim, was an action meant to spur Jesus on to use his miraculous powers to defend himself and so hasten the moment when the kingdom of God would be ushered in.

This theory is impossible to defend in the light of what the Scriptures say about Judas. Jesus refers to him as 'the one doomed to destruction' (John 17:12). But this theory does hold a warning for those followers of Christ who grow impatient with what they see as a lack of progress. There is always the tendency with some to try to force the pace and in doing so to introduce schemes and methods which do not glorify Jesus. It is possible to organize results, and if we are only interested in results there will be a temptation to do this. If we preach a way of salvation that is less than the biblical way, many may accept it and make a profession of faith, but it will not be true saving faith. If we ignore the New Testament call for repentance and substitute instead an easy-believism, the results may well be spectacular, but God will not be honoured and people will be lulled into a false sense of security. If we make salvation the answer to problems of human relationships instead of salvation from personal sin and guilt, our message will be a popular one, but it will not be the gospel. All of this is no less a betrayal of Jesus and his gospel than was Judas' kiss.

The motives behind such actions may sometimes be selfless and commendable, but if they bypass the glory and majesty of Christ in the gospel, they are in fact a betrayal. We can betray Christ without having sinister motives, and all Christians should beware of this. If we are not satisfied with the gospel as revealed in the Scriptures and seek to make amendments to it in order to make it more palatable to sinners, then we are betraying divine revelation and no good can come from it.

Foreordained

Was Judas foreordained to betray Jesus and therefore merely a helpless pawn in the plan of God? If he was 'doomed to destruction', can he be blamed for what he did? If his actions were carried out 'so that the Scriptures would be fulfilled', surely he cannot be held responsible because he could have done nothing else?

How do we deal with such arguments? Man is responsible for his own sins and cannot hide behind foreordination. Judas, like Pontius Pilate and Herod, 'did what
[God's] power and will had decided beforehand should
happen' (Acts 4:28), but God none the less held them
accountable. John Brown argues that 'The divine fore-
knowledge and prediction of events does not affect their
moral character. Judas is not the less guilty, nor his punishment less severe, that by his treachery a divine purpose
was fulfilled, a divine prediction accomplished.'[1]

J. C. Ryle tells us, 'It shows the desperate hopelessness
of anyone who, living in great light and privileges like Judas, misuses his opportunities, and deliberately follows the
bent of his own sinful inclinations.'[2]

Men have become ingenious in their attempts to excuse sin, but God is not fooled. We, like Judas, have to
answer for our own sins, and it will be no use pleading
that we could not help acting as we did. It will be useless to
plead a poor upbringing, lack of privileges, or even ignorance, to excuse our sins. Each one will have to give an
account for his or her own actions. Every Judas will, sooner
or later, be exposed. The mask may fall off, or be torn off,
when the person least expects it, but off it will come.

Brazen sin

Having decided to betray Jesus, Judas, with an obstinate
brazenness, still gathered with Jesus and the apostles. He

did not separate himself from them, but continued as if nothing had changed. But Jesus knew, and in the upper room the Saviour took great pains to minister to Judas. When Jesus spoke of betrayal all the other apostles were disturbed, afraid that they might be the betrayer. Judas had no such fears. They asked, 'Surely not I, Lord?' The thought that they could be the guilty one appalled each of the eleven. Judas repeated the same words to Jesus but felt nothing of the anguish and grief of the other apostles. None of the solemn events of the Last Supper appears to have touched Judas. Instead he brazened it out. John Brown says, 'It would appear that Judas had carried his effrontery and hypocrisy so far, as not only to have come to the feast, but to have taken for himself a place near his Master as a trusted disciple, and one who deserved to be trusted.'[3]

This man had rejected all he had seen and experienced of Jesus over the past three years, and by now he seems to have been immune to the love of Jesus. So it is not surprising to read, 'Satan entered into him' (John 13:27). When a man rejects the light and love of Christ, he leaves the way wide open for Satan to direct his actions. Judas had set his mind to betray Jesus before Satan entered him. He could no more blame Satan for what he did than he could blame divine foreordination. If we play with sin it will finish up playing with us. If we tolerate 'small' sins, then in time we shall be happy with the grossest of sins.

Judas must be one of the most tragic figures in the New Testament. To be so close to Jesus and yet never to understand him is amazing. This man was as two-faced as it is possible to be. He did not just betray Jesus, but he did it with a kiss. There were other ways he could have identified the Saviour to the soldiers, but he chose to do it with a kiss. Even in the act of betrayal he was pretending to love Jesus.

John MacArthur says:

> Judas's particular act of betrayal and its direct consequences were unique, but his basic attitude toward Jesus is characteristic of every false believer. Every age has found Judases in the church, those who outwardly feign allegiance to Christ but who at heart are his enemies. They identify themselves with the church for many different reasons, but all of the reasons are self-serving. Whether it be to get ahead in business by appearing respectable, to gain social acceptance by being religious, to salve a guilty conscience by means of pretended righteousness, or to accomplish any other purpose, the underlying motive is always to serve and please self, not God.
>
> Judas is the archetype of Christ-rejecters and the supreme example of wasted privilege and opportunity. He is the picture of those who love money, having forsaken the priceless Son of God for thirty pieces of silver. He is the classic hypocrite, who feigned love and loyalty for Christ even as he delivered him up for execution. He is the supreme false disciple, the son of Satan who masquerades as a son of God.[4]

Questions for personal thought or group discussion

1. Do you feel sorry for Judas? Was he a helpless pawn caught up in affairs beyond his control?
2. In what ways can we betray Christ today?
3. Is it possible to become immune to the love of Jesus?
4. Discuss the quotation from John McArthur at the end of the chapter.

7.

Not for sale

Acts 8:9-25

Without question the greatest delusion anyone can have is to think he that he is saved when in fact he is not. Simon the Sorcerer in Acts 8 fooled himself with this delusion and for a while the church was also deceived, but God was never fooled by it.

Simon was one of the most prominent men in Samaria. Clearly he had an exalted opinion about himself: 'He boasted that he was someone great' (v. 9). The people agreed with him and thought of him as some kind of deity. They were impressed with his ability to perform magic and sorcery. What exactly this was we do not know, but it was impressive. Simon's self-esteem and public status depended upon this ability, so when Philip came to Samaria preaching and performing signs and wonders, Simon's standing in the community was threatened.

He was now not the only one with remarkable powers and it appeared that Philip's power was greater than Simon's, so Simon 'followed Philip everywhere, astonished by the great signs and miracles he saw' (v. 13). Simon the

Sorcerer was so impressed that he professed salvation and was baptized. Probably the Christians considered this an exciting happening. Here was one of the most powerful men in the city professing salvation and becoming a Christian. But it is clear from Acts 8 that Simon's attraction to Christianity was not caused by any conviction of personal sin, but by the professional interest of a magician in the abilities of someone whom he considered to be a rival.

What is salvation?

Salvation is not an interest, vague or serious, in some aspect of the gospel or church life. It is not the result of an accident of birth because no one can be born a Christian. Sadly, many people call themselves Christians on the strength of these two misconceptions. An attraction to the architecture of old church buildings, a love of church music, or perhaps a fascination with ceremony and ritual — all these things hold an importance and value for some folk. They are not interested in belief and doctrine; in fact such things bore them. Christianity for them is an external matter of things they like.

Others think they are Christians simply because they are born into a Roman Catholic, Anglican, or Baptist, family. They inherit the family religion in the same way they inherit the family possessions. Once again it is only an external faith with no conviction or substance.

Salvation is a matter of personal faith in Christ that is the result of a conviction of one's own sin and guilt. It is not a passing interest; it is not something casual; it is not inherited; but it is an all-consuming commitment to Christ that changes the life of the convert. There can be no salvation without repentance, and no repentance without conviction of sin. Salvation is from the guilt and consequences of our sin. It deals with spiritual matters and the effects are eternal.

Simon, we are told, believed and was baptized. These are both activities the New Testament urges upon sinners, but what did Simon believe? Did he believe he was a sinner under the wrath and judgement of the holy God? Did he see that his old life of self-esteem and magic was all wrong and needed to be repented of? Baptism cannot take away sin and therefore it cannot save. It is merely an outward sign of an inward work of grace that has already taken place. Sadly, it became apparent that Simon knew nothing of grace, for his 'heart [was] not right before God' (v. 21) and he was still 'captive to sin' (v. 23).

There are many in our churches who, like Simon, have made an outward profession of faith but lack the essential inward work of grace that alone saves. Such people can fool themselves and fool the church, but they do not fool God.

Not for sale

Simon's true spiritual condition was revealed when Peter and John came to Samaria. They prayed for the new converts and laid hands on them, and when they did so the Samaritan Christians received the Holy Spirit. Simon was greatly excited by this and wanted this power to add to his own repertoire of magic tricks, so he offered Peter and John money if they would tell him how it was done.

Peter's response was devastating as in a few sentences he exposed Simon as the sorcerer who still had no concept of salvation: 'May your money perish with you …! You have no part or share in this ministry, because your heart is not right before God' (v. 20). Simon, for all his profession and baptism, knew nothing of God. He thought of God in the same way as he thought of his magic abilities. He did not understand that nothing God has is for sale. If a man thinks he can buy salvation, or perhaps earn it by his own efforts, he is revealing a total ignorance as to the holiness of God and the depths of his own sin.

Simon's problem was that he was still completely absorbed in signs and wonders. He saw them as a means to continue being somebody special. In fact he had no desire to change what he was, only to establish his old position more firmly. He was not concerned about salvation, only about self-esteem and position. For him, signs and wonders were a means to that end.

True salvation

Peter showed Simon what was spiritually wrong with him and what he needed to do in order to become a Christian.

Get right with God

The first thing that Peter told him was: 'Your heart is not right before God' (v. 21). This was true of Simon, and it is true of everyone who has not repented of their sin and trusted in Christ alone for salvation. The Bible has some devastating things to say about the human heart:

- The heart is deceitful above all things and beyond cure (Jeremiah 17:9).
- For out of the heart come evil thoughts, murder, adultery, sexual immorality, theft, false testimony, slander. These are what make a man unclean (Matthew 15:19).

It is our sin that makes us unacceptable to God and nothing else will change this unless we repent.

Repent

Secondly, Peter told Simon, 'Repent of this wickedness' (Acts 8:22). Repentance is not a case of trying your best to put right all the sin there is in your life. Repentance means that the sinner, conscious of his guilt, and aware of the mercy of God in Christ, turns from his sin to God. The repentant sinner knows a loathing and a hatred of sin and a great desire to live in obedience to God. He will cry to God for mercy and pardon.

Repentance means more than being sorry for your sins. It is possible to be sorry for the trouble and distress that sin has caused you without giving the slightest thought to what your sin has done to God. By the work of the Holy Spirit, sin is seen for what it really is: not just a character defect, but a permanent state of rebellion against the love and care and righteous authority of a holy God. It is this new understanding of God and of one's own sin that leads to true repentance. There will be a great desire to break with the past and to live in future only to please God. That is repentance.

Pray for forgiveness

Finally, Peter urged Simon, 'Pray to the Lord. Perhaps he will forgive you' (v. 22). The prayer for forgiveness of sin is not a polite petition but a cry of desperation. Salvation becomes the most important thing in one's life. An urgency is created in our hearts by the Holy Spirit that will know no relief until salvation comes. It is the Lord alone who can forgive sin, so it is to him alone that the repentant sinner goes.

Whether Simon did this or not we are not told, but the New Testament does tell us that when we come to Christ in repentance and faith, he will receive us and forgive us all our sin. This is true salvation. It is not a fascination with miracles or anything else, but a soul made right with God through the merit and grace of the Lord Jesus Christ.

Questions for personal thought or group discussion

1. Do you know anyone who made a profession of faith which turned out to be false? How can you help such people to come to true faith?
2. Does it matter what a person believes?
3. How can a sinner get right with God?
4. If Simon had been truly converted what would have been the signs of that in his life?

8.

'You fool!'

Luke 12:13-21

In this chapter we consider a man whom God himself called a fool. In the parable of the rich fool in Luke 12, the man makes no direct attempt to fool God, but his whole thinking epitomizes an attitude that treats God as being unimportant in comparison with material possessions.

The parable is the answer of Jesus to a man in the crowd who had been listening to his preaching. Jesus had been teaching great spiritual truths — the seriousness of divine judgement (v. 5), the value God puts on human beings (v. 7) and the ministry of the Holy Spirit (v. 10). Here were great truths preached by the greatest preacher ever. Then suddenly Jesus was interrupted: 'Someone in the crowd said to him, "Teacher, tell my brother to divide the inheritance with me" ' (v. 13).

In the midst of a great spiritual sermon here is a man worried about money. He thought he was being cheated by his brother and wanted Jesus to act as a mediator. Clearly he had not been listening to anything Jesus had been saying, because there is no relationship between his request and the content of the sermon. How many hearers of the gospel are just like this man? They hear the Word of God but their minds are occupied with other concerns. Even the preaching of Jesus could not gain this man's attention.

Whether the man's complaint was just or not is unimportant and Jesus deals with him rather curtly: 'Man, who appointed me a judge or an arbiter between you?' He is in effect saying, 'This is not my business. My business is with much more important matters.' Jesus immediately goes on to warn against the sin of greed and to make the declaration that 'A man's life does not consist in the abundance of his possessions.' To illustrate this he tells the parable of the rich fool.

It is true that God is concerned about every part of our lives. Nothing about us is unimportant to God. Jesus taught this earlier in the chapter when he told us that the very hairs on our head are all numbered. But we have to keep things in proportion. There are issues much more important than material possessions. Life is more than money and position. If we think that God has the same scale of values as we do, then this parable is crucial for us.

A foolish man

The man Jesus brings before us in the parable appears to have had many very commendable qualities. As far as we can tell, he was diligent, hard-working, honest and astute. But God is interested in more than upright living. One year this rich man had a remarkable harvest. So much was produced on his land that his barns were filled to overflowing and still large quantities of produce were left over. All this was the result of his skill as a farmer. He had worked hard for it and come by it honestly. But he had a problem. What was he going to do in order to store all that his land had produced? He decided there was only one thing to do. He would have to expand. He would have a crash building programme, pull down the old barns and erect new, bigger ones.

This was good business sense. If he sought the advice of his friends they would probably have all agreed that this was a wise thing to do. They would have admired him, praised him and some would have envied him. His own opinion was a sort of smug satisfaction. He thought he could now retire comfortably, take life easy and enjoy his wealth. But God said, 'You fool!' The man whom other people admire and envy, God calls a fool.

He was a fool because he confused his soul with his stomach. Life for him consisted only of bodily needs and comforts. He said to himself, 'Soul, you have many goods laid up for many years' (v. 19, NKJV). Here is an appalling picture of how millions of people live. Here is a thoroughly materialistic man who imagines that his soul can be fed with material things. He has no sense of the eternal value of his soul. He lives for the present and has no thought of God.

There are many people, rich and poor, who live according to the same philosophy. They live and plan as if this world was all there is. Possessions and present comfort

are all that concern them and they live as if there were no
death, no judgement and no world to come. The farmer
in the parable thought in terms of many years, but God
called him a fool and said, 'Tonight you will die, and then
what will happen to your riches?'

True riches

The Bible does not condemn riches, but it does clearly
warn against the dangerous influences money can have
on people. Wealth tends to trap us into materialism and
insensitivity to others. It is not money, but the love of
money, that is the root of all evil. This is why Jesus said
that it is easier for a camel to go through the eye of a
needle than for a rich man to enter the kingdom of God.

   This does not mean that no rich people can be saved.
The Scriptures and church history tell us of believers who
were rich and show us how they used their possessions for
the glory of God. Such people can, in the providence of
God, have an important part to play in the spreading of
the gospel. The Countess of Huntingdon, for example, used
her great wealth and her social position to help the ministry of George Whitefield and other eighteenth-century
preachers.

   The problem is that riches can become the all-consuming passion of life, and that is foolish because, as Jesus
says in the parable, death will separate us from all our
possessions. Two men were discussing the death of a

millionaire and one asked, 'How much did he leave?' His friend answered, 'Everything.' That is true of us all. We cannot take it with us, so why do we value possessions so much? It is because the world is real to us and heaven is not, and this is because God is not real to us.

Riches can give us prominence, power and position in this world, but these things do not impress God. True riches are only to be found in God. A man who is rich towards God is truly rich. Inflation and money markets cannot touch his wealth. Thieves cannot steal it and death cannot snatch it away. In fact, death gives him more. Riches like this are only found in Christ.

Jesus describes true riches as being 'rich towards God' (v. 21). A man who is rich towards God has what Jesus calls 'treasure in heaven'. This is not 'pie in the sky when you die', but a very present reality because it delivers us from anxiety. It is interesting that as soon as Jesus finishes telling the parable, his application in verse 22 is to tell us not to worry about possessions. According to Jesus, the cause of worry is having your treasure in the wrong place: 'Where your treasure is, there your heart will be also' (v. 34). By 'treasure' he means the things we value most. In the parable the rich man valued only those things that could not leave earth. Such an attitude always produces anxiety.

People say that they want enough money so that they will have no worries. But the problem is that the more possessions we gather in order to feel secure, the more we feel we need these things in order to keep and protect our security. The result is uncertainty and no security. It is foolishness because wealth cannot buy happiness. Jesus said that happiness depends upon being rich towards God.

Contrast this with the 'health-and-wealth' teaching of today. Instead of delivering us from a fascination with the world's treasures, this teaching encourages us to seek them. We can then fall into the trap of measuring God's blessing in terms of material prosperity. But Jesus tells us that the marks of God's blessing are poverty of spirit, mourning for personal sin and persecution for righteousness' sake. Real spirituality is not seen in health and wealth, but in being rich towards God.

Rich towards God

To be rich towards God means to have one's priorities right. Immediately after warning against anxiety over material things (vv. 22-30), Jesus tells us to seek first God's kingdom. This does not mean that we live in a material cloud cuckoo land, sitting down idly and saying, 'The Lord will provide.' We have to face our responsibilities in terms of food and clothing, but we face them with trust in God. That removes worry and helps us to give our priority to seeking spiritual refreshment.

Even more than this, being rich towards God means that we live here and now in anticipation of the coming of the Lord and of future glory (vv. 35-40). If our treasure is in heaven, our hearts will also be there and we shall look forward eagerly to the time when the whole of our being will be there. For such a person, death can only increase his riches.

The problem with the rich fool was that he was not rich enough to die. He had an enormous debt that he was totally incapable of paying. God is not impressed with our bank balance. His eye is focused on the debt of sin which we have all incurred. Every time we sin, we break the law of God and that act is noted in heaven. The debt grows, and it has to be paid if we are to escape hell.

It is one of the most amazing things in the world how intelligent men can so easily distort the thinking and words of God to suit themselves. By any standards Cecil Rhodes was a great man. He was a statesman, financier and empire-builder, but he said that he was never sure that God existed. He then decided to give God the benefit of the doubt and from then on, he claimed, he lived his life to do the will of God — which he evidently considered was to make the world English! Such arrogance and stupidity are mind-boggling, and the opinions of great men often sway the world. But they do not fool God.

All men, rich or poor, need Jesus because he alone is able to pay the debt our sin has incurred. The message of the gospel is that God made Jesus responsible for the sin of all whom he came to save and on the cross the Saviour died in their place paying their debt. This act of atonement is the only thing that can make guilty sinners right with God. Nothing else, whether it be riches, position or power, impresses God.

Questions for personal thought or group discussion

1. How do you think it could be possible for a person to hear Jesus preach and yet not benefit from it?
2. Can you think of any other parables which Jesus told to deal directly with the attitude of his hearers?
3. Why was the man in the parable a fool? What was so foolish about his actions?
4. What does it mean to have your treasure in heaven?

9.

Lying to God

Acts 5:1-16

The church in the Acts of the Apostles faced serious opposition from the Jewish religious authorities. They were forbidden to preach the gospel, which must be the most severe restriction that could possibly be placed on a group of believers. But the opposition strengthened rather than weakened the church. They were thrown totally upon the mercies of God. Not for a moment did they consider stopping preaching the message of Jesus. They knew there would be a price to pay for their faithfulness to God, but this did not deter them. They sought God in prayer, not because they did not know what to do, but to ask for strength and boldness to do what they knew had to be done. God answered: 'After they prayed, the place where they were meeting was shaken. And they were all filled with the Holy Spirit and spoke the word of God boldly' (Acts 4:31).

This greatly encouraged the Christians and their church life was enriched with a warm and generous spirit in telling unbelievers the truth, and with a deep concern for each other's needs. The fact that 'All the believers were one in

heart and mind' (Acts 4:32) is a great testimony to the
reality of the faith of those first Christians. But even among
such people there were those who were not in tune with
the majority of the church. A married couple named
Ananias and Sapphira were guilty of the grossest hypocrisy which eventually resulted in their death.

These two sold some land and pretended to give all the
proceeds to the church. Together they had concocted a
plan to gain praise for themselves without having to sacrifice too much money. Their hypocrisy was exposed by
Peter, who accused them of lying to God. The exposure
was too much for them and they both collapsed and died.

Two questions

Two questions come out of the story in Acts 5. Were
Ananias and Sapphira true Christians, and was the punishment for their sin too severe?

There has always been a difference of opinion among
Christians as to whether or not Ananias and Sapphira were
true believers. Some point to Simon the Sorcerer in Acts 8
to show that no church, whether in New Testament times
or since, can guarantee that every single one of its members at any given time is a true Christian. This is obviously
right, but it is interesting to compare the words Peter uses
to Ananias and Sapphira with those which he addresses to
Simon. To Simon he says, 'Your heart is not right before
God,' clearly indicating that this man was not saved. There
is no such indication in his words to Ananias and his wife.

But some would object that no true Christian could have his heart filled by Satan. Peter, from his own experience, would know that this is not true (Matthew 16:21-23).

So was the profession of faith made by Ananias and Sapphira false? Had they deceived the church with their claim to be Christians? If that was the case then their sin of lying to God would not perhaps have been too surprising. In any case, all believers are capable of committing just about any sin. The New Testament nowhere seeks to hide the possibility of true Christians falling into sin and numerous examples are given of the sins of God's people.

Whether they were Christians or not does not affect the crucial lesson this story puts before us. Their death was not the result of Peter's putting them under pressure. Dr Lloyd-Jones, preaching on Acts 5, put it like this: 'This is a judicial action on the part of God… God does something to lay down a great principle. God gives an indication to his own people as to who he is and how he acts.'

This incident has to be seen as one aspect of Satan's attack upon the church. The opposition of the Jews was not weakening the church, so Satan attacked from within. Peter recognized this when he said, 'Ananias, how is it that Satan has so filled your heart that you have lied to the Holy Spirit …?' Clearly, Ananias had been very severely tempted by Satan, but it was his responsibility to withstand that. The sin could not be blamed on Satan but on Ananias and his wife. In dealing severely with this sin God was demonstrating his opposition to all the works of Satan, whether in the world or in the church. Christians have to see that each one has a responsibility for keeping the church pure. This lesson was learnt, and 'Great fear seized the whole church' (v. 11). The next verses (vv. 12-16) also show that great and, indeed, exceptional blessing came to the church once the sin of its members had been dealt with.

What if God had not dealt with this sin? Ananias and Sapphira would have succeeded in fooling the church. They would have gained for themselves a reputation for godliness that was undeserved. Perhaps Ananias would have been made one of the leaders of the church, like Barnabas, who had also sold land and given the money to the church. The consequences of placing Ananias in a position of leadership could have been disastrous. But God intervened and stopped the matter at its inception.

Hypocrisy

Fooling the church is not too difficult, but fooling God is impossible. If God does not deal with us today in exactly the same manner as he dealt with Ananias and Sapphira, he still does deal with our hypocrisy. This is a sin that Jesus particularly despised. In the Sermon on the Mount he speaks powerfully against it (Matthew 6:1-6,16-18).

Some writers have likened Ananias' sin to that of Achan in Joshua 7. Achan was responsible for the defeat for God's people. Blessing was withheld from the whole nation because of the sin of this one man. Is the same thing happening today in our churches? Could it be that the hypocrisy of a few is holding back blessing?

We need to realize that as Christians we cannot live for ourselves. Everything we do as believers affects other Christians, and this is particularly true in the local church. Directly or indirectly, we all influence each other for good or evil. God tells us that we are members of the body of Christ. We are part of the church, part of a fellowship.

Lies

It may be that we would never intentionally lie to God. But it has been pointed out how easy it is to lie in our hymn-singing. For instance, do we really mean it when we sing:

'Take my life, and let it be
Consecrated, Lord, to thee;
Take my moments and my days,
Let them flow in ceaseless praise…

'Take my silver and my gold,
Not a mite would I withhold…'?

Perhaps we think that hymns do not count. If that is so, what is the point in using them in worship? A hymn addressed to God is no different from a prayer. The answer is not to refuse to sing such hymns, but to order our lives so that they truly reflect the desires of our hearts.

Questions for personal thought or group discussion

1. Why does persecution strengthen rather than weaken the church?
2. Do you think Ananias and Sapphira were believers?
3. If God was to deal with our sins in the same way, what do you think would be the reaction in your church?
4. Why is hypocrisy such a deadly sin?

10.

The sin of a good man

2 Samuel 11:1-27

The sin of David with Bathsheba, and the murder of her husband Uriah to which it led, is one of the saddest stories in the Old Testament. This sin was not committed by some ungodly man who cared nothing for the Lord, but by a deeply spiritual man whom God himself described as 'a man after my own heart'. David had known heights of spiritual blessing and experience that most Christians can only dream about. He had written some of the most glorious and beautiful spiritual songs ever composed. Yet this man sinned in a most terrible way.

We acknowledge that no Christian is perfect and that all believers sin, but this sin of David's was no sudden flash of temper or moment of selfishness. It was deliberate adultery and scheming murder. We are not to stand in judgement with a superior 'holier-than-thou' attitude, but neither are we casually to accept sin as if it were just a moral hiccup. David was no inexperienced youngster, but a man of about fifty. Here is the sin of a good man and we have to ask how could David have done what he did.

In the wrong place

The story starts in 2 Samuel 11:1-2 with what appears to be a very casual happening. David did not go looking for trouble. He was just walking around on the roof of his palace and happened to see this beautiful woman bathing. It appears to have been merely a chance event. But this was not the case. There are two important points here: this man of God was in the wrong place and in the wrong frame of mind.

Nothing happens by chance in a believer's life. We believe in the providence of God which leads and guides us, but if we ignore that providence and go our own way, then we make ourselves prey to the devil's schemes and plans. At another time David might have seen Bathsheba bathing and turned his eyes away. He would have known the words of Job 31:1: 'I made a covenant with my eyes not to look lustfully at a girl.' Normally David would have been in full agreement with Job. But now, in the wrong place and in the wrong frame of mind, it was all tragically different.

The first verse of 2 Samuel 11 tells us that it was the time when kings went off to war. The king's army went to war but King David did not. The verse ends: 'But David remained in Jerusalem.' The 'but' implies that David should have been with his soldiers. A. W. Pink calls it the 'ominous "but"', noting the Spirit's disapproval of the king's conduct'.[1] David was in the wrong place. He had turned his eyes away from his God-given duty and indulged a desire for an easy life. He was relaxing when he should have been in the battle. He preferred the luxuries of the palace to the hardships of the battlefield; in other words, he was in the wrong frame of mind. Long before he saw Bathsheba he was in trouble.

Roger Ellsworth says of David, 'David allowed the fire of devotion to God to burn low. Sin is always born in a damp, chilly heart. Omission usually precedes commission. Let a Christian become careless about his church attendance, or let him become half-hearted when he is in church, and he has already set one foot on the slippery slope of sin. Let him become casual about his Bible-reading, or let him read mechanically, and he has already hung the welcome sign out for sin. Let him leave off praying, or pray without feeling, and he has already planted the seeds of disaster.'[2]

Resist temptation

This is very relevant for every Christian. None of us is so strong and experienced in the Christian life that we become immune to temptation and sin. We may think that we could never be guilty of adultery, but it has happened to a frightening number of evangelical ministers and believers in recent years. The moral climate of the day encourages it. What David saw as he looked down from his palace roof, a beautiful woman undressed, we can see on any beach in the summer. But we can also see what David saw in our own homes every day on the TV.

How are we to deal with such things? Let us remember that, although we live in days of moral and sexual slackness, God's standards have never wavered. He still says,

'You shall not commit adultery.' Temptation may be strong but grace is stronger. With every temptation there is always a way out (1 Corinthians 10:13). One sin usually leads to another. It did with David, and so Uriah died. Adultery always involves broken promises, lies, deceit and betrayal. No one, man or woman, is immune to this particular sin; it has to be fiercely resisted.

This we do by keeping ourselves involved in the battle. Make sure that at all times your mind is spiritually alert and not dozing in moral and religious laziness. Joseph faced the same sort of temptation with Potiphar's wife, and he ran away as fast as he could. Sometimes that is the only way to resist evil. But David did not run; he looked. It is sometimes said that David only did what any king of the time would have done. But he was not any king; he was God's chosen king. Clearly he had lost sight of this and forgotten who he was. He also forgot the mercies of God and consequently when Satan tempted him with Bathsheba's body, he fell.

Notice the progression of his fall. First of all, he saw Bathsheba. He could not be blamed for that, except for the fact that he should have been at the battle and not on the palace roof. He obviously liked what he saw and looked with a growing interest. This he can be blamed for. The covenant made with his eyes was well and truly buried. Lastly, he made enquiries about the woman and at that point the sin had become almost inevitable. But God was good to David and gave him a warning through one of his servants: 'Isn't this Bathsheba ... the wife of Uriah?' She was married and therefore out of bounds, but David took no notice. The awful condemnation of Scripture, that in this act of sin David despised the Lord, is recorded twice over (2 Samuel 12:9,10).

An inherent weakness

Sadly, this was no casual fall on David's part. There was a basic inherent weakness in him that he ignored and failed to deal with. In Deuteronomy 17, God laid down three specific rules for the man who would be king over his people:

- He must not acquire a great number of horses (v. 16).
- He must not accumulate large amounts of silver and gold (v. 17).
- He must not take many wives (v. 17).

David was meticulous in obeying two of these three commands. After battles he slew the captive horses and dedicated captured silver and gold to the work of the Lord. But on the deeper issue, on the matter that was not outside himself but inside him, when it came to women, he broke God's law. We read in 2 Samuel 5:13, 'David took more concubines and wives in Jerusalem.'

Twenty years before he saw Bathsheba the seeds of this sexual sin were being sown in his heart. It did not stop there and to cover up his sin he arranged the death of Uriah. Then, with almost blatant insensitivity, he married

Bathsheba. 'But the thing David had done displeased the LORD' (2 Samuel 11:27).

We all have inherent weaknesses. They may relate to sex, money, pride, ambition, or almost anything. If you are a Christian you will know what your weakness is. There are areas in your Christian life where there is no compromise, but is there an area where a particular sin is encouraged, fed, protected and defended? If so you will have found yourself having to cover up that sin with another and, rather than repenting, attempting to justify your sin.

God is not fooled because to him there is no such thing as secret sin. Everything is open to our God and sin always displeases him.

Questions for personal thought or group discussion

1. If David's sin was repeated in the church today, do you think we would be tempted to doubt that the person was truly a man of God?
2. Is it true that the devil finds work for idle hands to do?
3. Compare the story of David and Bathsheba with that of Joseph and Potiphar's wife.
4. What would you say is your inherent weakness?

11.

'You are the man!'

2 Samuel 12:1-25; Psalms 32; 51

David was now married to Bathsheba and the son born of his sin was rocking in a cradle in the palace. Every moment of every day there was this visible reminder to the king of what he had done. But there was no repentance. Everyone knew of the great evil David had done, but he was the king and could get away with it. It seemed that even God was not too concerned because heaven was silent on the matter. For a year there was no repentance and God left David in this condition.

Here we see a very spiritual man deep in the grip of his own sin and refusing to repent. It is not an unusual scene because we can all be like this. Our sin may not be as vile as David's, but the question is not one of the degree of sin, but how we deal with it. It appears that David was not prepared to deal with it. A year had gone by and in all probability another year would have come and gone without any response from the king.

How did David feel? What was he thinking? Did he think no one cared? God had said nothing, so perhaps God did not care either. David knew God well enough to know that this was not true. But as Christians we easily delude ourselves when guilty of sin and as time goes on the delusion gets stronger.

Psalms of experience

As David looked back over his year of defiance of God he wrote two psalms. Psalms 32 and 51 show us how he felt at this time.

He says in Psalm 32:3: 'When I kept silent, my bones wasted away through my groaning all day long.' Clearly he was not happy. He could not speak to God about his sin and so he could not speak to God about anything. He acknowledges in verse 4 that there was a sense of divine judgement upon him. This was nothing as direct as what he felt when Nathan confronted him, but still it was there. He had lost the joy of his salvation (Psalm 51:12). All this David felt, but he did nothing. Perhaps he thought there was little he could do. Uriah was dead and the baby was born. Nothing could change these things.

What is very clear is that David was not enjoying the fruit of his sin. The nineteenth-century preacher Alexander Maclaren said, 'David learned, what we all learn (and the holier a man is, the more speedily and sharply the lesson follows on the heels of his sin), that every transgression is a blunder, that we never get the satisfaction which we expect from any sin, or if we do, we get something with it which spoils it all. A nauseous drug is added to the exciting, intoxicating drink which temptation offers, and though its flavour is at first disguised by the pleasanter

God our Shepherd watches over his sheep. He goes after the strays and restores them. He heals their backslidings and continues to love them freely. So immediately after we are told, 'But the thing David had done displeased the LORD', the next verse says, 'The LORD sent Nathan to David' (2 Samuel 11:27; 12:1).

'You are the man!'

The baby had already been born, so it must have been about a year after the sin was committed that God sent Nathan to David. If David was tempted to think that God had overlooked his sin he was in for a rude awakening.

Nathan was a wise man. He did not go straight up to the king and read the riot act. There are times when that approach is necessary, but not here. David had lived with his sin for a year and could easily have reacted with violent indignation if confronted directly. So Nathan told him a story.

There were two men, one very rich and the other poor. The rich man had many sheep, but the poor man had only one pet lamb. A visitor came to the rich man and, rather than kill one of his many sheep to feed the guest, he stole the poor man's pet lamb and killed it for the meal.

David had no intimation of what Nathan was doing. There had been no repentance, even if he had been under conviction of sin, so he was still blind to the terrible nature of his actions. He was like the man in the Sermon on the

Mount who could clearly see the speck of sawdust in someone else's eye but could not see the plank in his own. So he was passionately angry against the rich man in Nathan's story and demanded that he be put to death. Isn't it strange that most of us are totally intolerant of the very sin in others of which we ourselves are guilty?

From his own mouth David had convicted himself and Nathan simply, but devastatingly, announced, 'You are the man!' This brought from the king the confession: 'I have sinned against the LORD.' At last he had come to repentance and the depth of this can be seen in Psalm 51. Repentance is always followed by forgiveness: 'The LORD has taken away your sin' (2 Samuel 12:13). Repentance is not an easy way out because even though there is forgiveness there are still consequences of sin which have to be borne: 'But because by doing this you have made the enemies of the LORD show utter contempt, the son born to you will die' (2 Samuel 12:14).

Repentance leads to forgiveness; this does not bypass the consequences of sin, but it does lead to restoration to the Lord: 'He went into the house of the LORD and worshipped' (2 Samuel 12:20).

No secrets from God

Nathan very strongly reminded David that there are no secret sins before God. It is utter foolishness to think that we can deceive God by our so-called 'secret sins'. We should always fear sin because it grieves the heart of God and robs us of the joy of our salvation. Sin will never do us any good. It may for a while give great pleasure; it may get you a better job and more money; it may help you avoid some troubles; but eventually it will rob you, impoverish you and make you as miserable as it is itself.

In many ways what was worse than David's sin was his refusal to repent. We all sin. That is not an excuse, but it is a fact. When God awakens your conscience flee to him in confession and repentance. Don't let Satan keep you in sin, and don't let the Evil One deceive you into thinking that your sin means you are finished for ever as a Christian. There is always forgiveness when there is repentance.

Questions for personal thought or group discussion

1. Why did David not repent of his sin until he was compelled to do so? Would we be right to question whether such a repentance was genuine?
2. What is the difference between repentance and conviction of sin?
3. What does it mean to keep short accounts with God and is it advisable?
4. How do you deal with serious sin in a fellow believer?

12.

'I don't believe that!'

Luke 16:19-31

The next four chapters are based on the parable Jesus told in Luke 16 of the rich man and Lazarus. The parable is important because it deals with vital issues which men and women like to think God does not treat seriously — things such as the immortality of the soul, heaven and hell, the final judgement and the crucial place of the Bible in salvation. All these have been made controversial, or perhaps more accurately, many people have rejected them with the statement: 'I don't believe that.' But man's rejections do not affect the way in which God runs the world he has created. A person may sincerely believe that there is no such place as hell, but that does not change the reality of hell.

God is not taken in by protestations of sincerity, or what we consider to be fair or unfair. It is about time we took God seriously.

What happens after someone dies?

Some say, 'Nothing at all.' We merely cease to exist because this life is all there is. Others say we all go to heaven because there is no such place as hell, and the God of love takes us all home to himself in heaven. Still others say we go to purgatory — a sort of halfway house between heaven and hell — until we are good enough to enter heaven.

These are interesting views held by various men and women, but they are not what Jesus says in the New Testament. The parable of the rich man and Lazarus is meant to tell us what happens when we die. Very clearly Jesus says that after death it is either heaven or hell for all of us. But, equally clearly, Jesus teaches that our eternal destination is decided before death. The Bible says, 'Man is destined to die once, and after that to face judgement' (Hebrews 9:27), but death and judgement are not a means of assessing whether or not a person is good enough for heaven. That issue is decided before death.

The judgement is the carrying out of divine justice upon the souls of men and women. Life is short, but it is not insignificant because in this life we are confronted with the living God and the demands he makes on all men and women. Heaven and hell, the eternal destinies of everyone, are being decided now by our attitude to, and our relationship with, the eternal God and his Son Jesus Christ.

The human soul

Men and women are unique among all of God's creation
because we are made in the image of God. This means
that when God made us he put something of the stamp of
his own character upon us. Unlike the rest of creation we
are made to know and enjoy God. God made us living
souls with a capacity for prayer and worship.

The human soul is that which makes us distinct from
every other created being, and that soul is immortal.
Loraine Boettner says, 'Immortality means the eternal,
continuous, conscious existence of the soul after the death
of the body.'[1] This is not a popular doctrine with some but
clearly it is what the Bible teaches.

Let us take just one example of this biblical teaching. In
the Old Testament Job asked a question that most men
and women have asked at some point in their lives: 'If a
man dies, will he live again?' (Job 14:14). A person does
not have to be particularly religious to ask this question.
Perhaps the death of a loved one causes him or her to
consider eternity for a moment and the question then becomes quite natural. The answer Job discovers to the question is, sadly, one that not everyone finds. He says:

I know that my Redeemer lives,
    and that in the end he will stand upon the earth.
And after my skin has been destroyed,
    yet in my flesh I will see God

(Job 19:25-26).

The answer to the question is a most positive, 'Yes'. But the answer depends very much upon the individual's relationship with the Redeemer. Job was anticipating the words of Jesus the Redeemer when he said, 'I am the resurrection and the life. He who believes in me will live, even though he dies; and whoever lives and believes in me will never die' (John 11:25-26).

This is too much for some to believe but Boettner has a very simple illustration. Before the year 1492 many people thought that there might be land beyond the ocean. Others thought the world was flat and that there was no land beyond the horizon. People on the coast of Portugal or Spain could have looked out to the ocean believing that there was land over there, but they could not prove it. Then in 1492 Christopher Columbus sailed out, reached that land and came back with proof of the existence of a New World. Now there was proof because someone had been there and come back.

In the same way Jesus by his resurrection has proved what many people only hoped for. He has been there and come back. He died, but death could not hold him. Some people say that they would believe in life after death if someone came back from the dead, but they ignore the fact that someone already has. What greater proof can there be than the resurrection of Jesus Christ from the grave? Sadly, many people do not want to believe even with this proof, but the Christian's hope is in Christ. The Lord Jesus has been there and come back. He has conquered death.

Heaven or hell?

The human body is not immortal, but the soul is, and it
will have an eternal existence in either heaven or hell. There
is no biblical alternative to these two places. The concept
of purgatory is not found in Scripture. At death the body
goes to the grave and the soul to either heaven or hell.
Death is the separation of body and soul, but the Bible
also teaches of a resurrection when the body and soul of a
Christian are reunited and made suitable for heaven.

In the parable Jesus does not start with the deaths of
the two men, but he first tells us something about their
lives. The two could not have been more different. One
was exceptionally rich and lived in luxury, while the other
was a beggar who lived in abject poverty. But that was not
the deciding factor as to whether they went to heaven or
hell. The rich man did not go to hell just because he was
rich. Abraham was rich and so was Joseph, yet they both
went to heaven. Neither did Lazarus go to heaven simply
because in this life he had a rough time. This point has to
be made because there are some people who think the
unfairness of life here and now will all be put right in the
next life.

Brownlow North, who wrote a book on this parable,
gives an illustration of two people he met who were living
in extreme poverty in the middle of the nineteenth century. These two, a man and a woman, were convinced
that they were going to heaven simply because they were
poor. They were absolutely sure that because they had it

terribly hard in this life, when death came they would go
to heaven and the afterlife would rectify all the problems
of this life. Brownlow North sought to show them that they
had no hope in death without Christ. They would not listen to him and had it fixed firmly in their minds that just
because they were poor they were going to heaven. Both
these people died without Christ, and whatever trials and
tribulations they had in this life were as nothing compared
to the hell to which they were going without Christ as their
Saviour.

The deciding factor

What decides whether we go to heaven or hell is not our
financial position but our relationship to the Lord God.
There is nothing in the parable that condemns the rich
man for being rich, or praises Lazarus because he was
poor. The rich man's problem was not his bank balance
but his attitude. We are told that he 'was dressed in purple
and fine linen and lived in luxury every day'. This is not
merely a description of wealth, but of opulence and ex-
travagance, of a man completely wrapped up in himself.
Apparently fine linen was worth six times its weight in gold
and purple cloth was extremely expensive. His riches did
not create his attitude; they merely served to demonstrate
his self-centred, godless attitude to life. He saw the need
of Lazarus, who begged at his gate, but had no sympathy
and offered no help.

Such an attitude can dominate lives that do not have wealth. You can be poor and yet have great desire for riches so that you could satisfy your selfish ambitions. Several years ago the newspapers reported on a group of cleaners who worked in the same hotel. They had a football pools syndicate and each week the cleaners contributed to it, and sent their coupon away in the hope that one day they would all be rich. Every week they filled in exactly the same set of numbers and there was great excitement one week when these numbers turned out to be the correct ones. This meant they had won £700,000. But then they discovered that that very week the woman who sent in the coupon had filled in a different set of numbers. You can imagine their anger. They refused to talk to this woman. They had worked together for years, but now they would have nothing to do with her. As far as they were concerned, she had robbed them of £700,000 and they would probably go on being bitter for the rest of their lives.

Their attitude to life is very much like that of the man in the parable. You can be poor and envy the rich, and it is all because God has no place in your life. Such an attitude leads to hell, and a person's bank balance has very little to do with it.

What was Lazarus' attitude to God and to life? Remember that this is a parable and Jesus wants to teach us certain lessons. It has to be significant, therefore, that he gives the poor man a name. The name Lazarus means, 'God has helped.' Surely Jesus means us to see that here was a man who, though living in the most appalling conditions, trusted God and looked to God for help. His attitude to God is reflected in his attitude towards other things. He did not envy the rich man and would have been quite content with the crumbs from his table. All he wanted was enough to keep him alive. Here was a man who, though completely dependent upon others, had no bitterness and trusted God. He could have been resentful and full of self-pity, but he was not. God was his helper. His heart was right with God, and that is why he went to heaven.

Questions for personal thought or group discussion

1. What do you think happens when a person dies?
2. What do you think of the popular belief that we make our own hell? How does this fit in with the biblical teaching on hell?
3. Discuss Boettner's definition of immortality.
4. Is the body immortal as well as the soul?

13.

Death and hell

Luke 16:19-31; Romans 1:18-32

Jesus tells us that the rich man died and went to hell. Lazarus also died, so death is no respecter of person or position. All men, rich or poor, have to die. No one will argue with this, but why is it so? Why do we have to die?

Three kinds of death

What is death? The Bible speaks of three kinds of death, spiritual, physical and eternal. The answer to the question, 'What is death?' has to bear these three aspects of death in mind.

Spiritual death is the separation of the soul from God. That is what happened to Adam in Genesis 3 when he sinned. God had said to Adam and Eve that if they ate of the fruit of one particular tree, they would die. They did eat and they died immediately. It is true that their bodies still continued to function in the same way as before, but they died spiritually the moment they sinned against God. They died to God. The soul was separated from God, and that is now the natural condition of every human being. We are spiritually dead.

Boettner says, 'Spiritual death, like a poisoned fountain, pollutes the whole stream of life, and were it not for the restraining influence of common grace ordinary human life would become a hell on earth.'[1] Spiritual death is God's immediate judgement on sin. We are all sinners; therefore we are all spiritually dead. This means we are unable to appreciate and enjoy God. The image of God in which we were made is shattered and now, 'The mind of sinful man is death … the sinful mind is hostile to God. It does not submit to God's law, nor can it do so. Those controlled by the sinful nature cannot please God' (Romans 8:6-8). This condition remains until the sinner is born again.

Physical death is the separation of the soul from the body. This is what we experience when we die.

Eternal death, says Boettner, 'is spiritual death made permanent'.[2] In other words, it is hell. It is the ultimate achievement of sin to damn souls to hell. Because this death is eternal, there is no end to it and no escape from it.

Everyone will experience physical death. Eternal death is the end of all those who do not have Jesus as their Saviour, and the only way to avoid it is to get the condition of spiritual death changed now in this life. Sin is the cause of death and therefore sin has to be dealt with.

Sin and death

Each of these three kinds of death is the product of sin. We are told in the Scriptures that death is the wages of sin; it is the inevitable consequence of sin. James tells us in his epistle that sin, when it has run its course, brings death. All men therefore die for the same reason. The vilest criminal and the most upright and respectable person will both die, and the reason in both cases will be exactly the same because the only explanation for death is sin.

When someone dies the law of the land requires a doctor to fill in a death certificate stating the cause of death. After due consideration he will write on the death certificate that the cause of death was a heart attack, cancer, pneumonia, or some other disease. But the real cause of death is sin. What the doctor puts on the death certificate is the means by which death comes to us. It is not the cause, merely the way by which death, which we have all earned by our sin, ushers us into the presence of the holy Judge.

All of us are by nature spiritually dead, but not all will die eternally. This is because Christ came into the world to deal with the problem of sin. In accepting the fact that we are all going to die physically, people come to the mistaken conclusion that there is nothing we can do about death. But the gospel says that if the problem of sin is dealt with so too is the problem of spiritual and eternal death.

New birth

As well as three kinds of death, the Bible also speaks of
two kinds of birth. There is a *physical birth* which all human
beings experience, but there is also something which Jesus
calls a spiritual or *new birth*. This is what Jesus is referring
to when he says we must all be born again. The objective
of the gospel is to defeat death, and it does this by provid-
ing for the sinner a new birth. Jesus explains this to us in
John 3 and he uses an Old Testament story to illustrate his
point.

The Israelites were on their way through the desert to
the promised land when they sinned against God. God
judged them then and there by sending poisonous snakes
into the camp. The snakes bit the people and many died.
They recognized the great peril they were in, and in their
anguish cried out to God to help them. God's reply was to
tell Moses to make a bronze snake and put it up on a pole,
so that if anyone was bitten and about to die from the
poison, they should look to the bronze snake and if they
did so, they would live (see Numbers 21:4-9).

This was God's way of dealing with the death that was
plaguing them because of their sin. Jesus drew the parallel
with his own work of saving sinners from eternal death:
'Just as Moses lifted up the snake in the desert, so the Son
of Man must be lifted up, that everyone who believes in
him may have eternal life. For God so loved the world
that he gave his only begotten Son, that whoever believes
in him shall not perish but have eternal life' (John 3:14-16).

Moses' action delivered the Israelites from physical death, but what Jesus did on the cross is to deliver his people from spiritual and eternal death. Bearing this in mind, we now come back to the parable. The rich man died and Lazarus died. Did they both die the same kind of death? Yes, on one level — in that in both cases the body was separated from the soul; but no in another sense, because the soul of one went to heaven and the soul of the other to hell.

Hell

There are several words in the original Bible languages that are translated as 'hell' in our English versions. The two most common in the New Testament are 'Hades' and 'Gehenna'. Generally 'Hades' means 'death', or 'the grave', but it is also sometimes used to mean the place of punishment. The rich man was in Hades where he was in torment. In the parable we are told he was in agony, in fire.

Gehenna in the New Testament *always* means the place of punishment. The word is derived from Ge-Hinnom, which was the name of a valley where the rubbish of Jerusalem was burnt. It was also associated with all sorts of sin and idolatry. This is the background to the word 'Gehenna' and it came to be used as the name of the place where sin was punished. Jesus uses this word eleven times in the New Testament to refer to hell. For instance, this is the word he uses when he says, 'If your hand causes you to sin, cut it off. It is better for you to enter life maimed than with two hands to go into hell, where the fire never goes out' (Mark 9:43).

Hell is where God deals with man in his sin. To be in hell is to be in the presence of God without a Saviour and therefore without hope. There is no pleasure in hell. It is not a place where sinners can enjoy their sin without restraint. It is the place where sin is punished. In the Scriptures, fire is used to describe hell, but this is only a picture. Hell is far more terrible than our minds can grasp. But perhaps the most terrible thing about hell is that it is endless. Spurgeon said in one sermon that on every link in every chain in hell is stamped the inscription 'for ever'.

The rich man was in hell and he was there not because he was rich, but because he was a sinner who had no Saviour to deal with his sin. There are men and women in hell who have spent every Sunday of their adult life in church, and there are those in hell who have never entered a church. There are people in hell who have lived moral and upright lives in this world, and there are also those in hell who have lived the most wicked and degrading lives this world has ever seen. Why then does someone go to hell? Because that person's sin has not been dealt with by the love and grace of God in Christ. All you have to do to go to hell is to go on ignoring God and ignoring the gospel of the Lord Jesus Christ. Every one of us is by nature in a state of spiritual death and, unless God in his grace makes us alive in Christ this will inevitably lead, via physical death, to eternal death. Do nothing, and go to hell.

The only hope

The only hope of a sinner's escaping hell is by believing and receiving the gospel of the Lord Jesus Christ. The word 'gospel' means 'good news', and could there ever be better news for a hell-deserving sinner than that God has provided a way of salvation for him? The gospel way is an infallible way because it is God's way. God is the Judge before whom we all have to stand. His holiness and his law condemn us, but he has provided a way by which the condemnation is removed for all who have received the new birth and are trusting in Christ alone for salvation. God the Judge has provided the remedy and he will surely accept his own answer.

Sinners can escape hell by fleeing to Christ to have their sins forgiven. The new birth that Jesus accomplishes for us by his death in our place on the cross removes spiritual death and deals with our sinful nature. Physical death then becomes, not the door to eternal death and hell, but merely the stepping-stone to eternal life and heaven. New birth removes spiritual death. We still have to face physical death, but for the Christian it has lost its sting and power. It is not now a step into the darkness of utter hopelessness and condemnation, but into the light and glory of the eternal God.

Two men died; one went to heaven and the other to hell. Where are you going? You may plead that you don't believe in hell, so this does not concern you. But whatever you believe now, the time will come when you will believe in hell. There are no unbelievers in hell, but by then it is too late.

Questions for personal thought or group discussion

1. What is the difference between spiritual death and physical death?
2. What is the difference between the *means* by which death comes and the *cause* of death?
3. How does the gospel teach that death can be defeated?
4. Why are people so willing to believe in heaven and so unwilling to believe in hell?

14.

A soul in hell

Luke 16:19-31; Matthew 24:36-51

This parable of Jesus is the only place in the Bible where we are shown a glimpse of the thoughts and emotions of a soul in hell. It is sometimes asked, 'What does a man have to do to go to hell? What terrible sin would have to be committed before a soul is damned for all eternity?' The simple answer of the Bible is that a person does not have to *do* anything to go to hell. We are born in sin and under the judgement of God and if we continue through life like that, then death will most surely usher us into hell.

In the matter of sin, both the rich man and Lazarus had the same start in life. Economically and socially their start in life could not have been more different, but spiritually and in terms of their relationship to God, their start was exactly the same. All men and women, whether rich or poor, clever or dull, black or white, are born with a sinful nature. It doesn't matter what a person's background is or what nation he or she comes from, every single one of us is born in a state of rebellion against God and under his condemnation.

This was not the reason, however, why the rich man was in hell. Lazarus had the same spiritual start but he was in heaven. The rich man's problem was that he was content to live without God. He never sought God, or wanted to know God. There are millions like this today. Their appetites and view of life never rise above the material and temporal.

Religious blindness

A Christian who had just come out of hospital was lamenting that the only thing the men in his ward talked about and lived for was to get out of hospital in order to go to the pub. Literally men were dying in that ward but the chief concern of most of them was that they were missing their pub.

Even worse than that is the fact that the average church attender is no different. Many are content with an outward form of religion and no real experience of God. It is not unusual to hear religious people declare that the 'God' they believe in would never send anyone to hell. They say that their 'God' is not the angry God of the Old Testament, but the loving, forgiving God whom Jesus talked about. He is the Father of all mankind and we are all his children; therefore there is no such place as hell, and everyone, irrespective of their beliefs and actions, will go to heaven.

Such a concept of a harmless, affable 'God' would be a great comfort to any unrepentant sinner, but unfortunately

for them this 'God' is not real. He is not the God of the
Bible. He is not the God and Father of the Lord Jesus
Christ. He is merely the creation of the mind of man and is
far removed from the true God whom Jesus revealed to
us. In the parable of the rich man and Lazarus, Jesus himself shows us the reality of hell and the condition of a soul
in that awful place.

Torment

This is a parable, so we have to be careful not to interpret
everything literally. The purpose of a parable is usually to
teach us a few basic truths. Christ would not have us interpret every detail here literally, but there are certain clear
pictures that emerge from this parable. First of all, note the
words Jesus uses. He says the soul in hell was in torment,
in agony and in fire. This tells us that hell is not some cosy
place where men can enjoy their sin unhindered. It is amazing how many people think this, but there is no freedom to
sin without impunity in hell. Sin there is forever being justly
punished. God deals with man's sin and the devil's sin
there. The devil is not the lord of hell; God is. The devil is
cast there in the same way that the rich man and all unrepentant sinners are cast there. Hell is not the domain of
Satan. It is the place where Satan is judged. There his sin,
and all sin, faces the wrath of God in all its fierceness.

Therefore, words like 'torment' and 'agony' are inevitable in order to describe hell, but is it just, is it right, that
this should be the case? Sin deserves hell, and sinners

deserve hell because in their lifetime they have gone on rejecting the love and grace and mercy of God. The word 'fire' is in fact an inadequate picture to describe the torments and horrors of hell. None of the words the Bible uses could adequately describe the torment of this place where men face the wrath of God.

In the parable we are told of something which added to the agony endured by the rich man in hell. From hell he saw Lazarus in heaven. He saw something that he had never seen before. He was experiencing something now in hell that he had never experienced in life — he could see into heaven. His torment was, therefore, not merely physical but emotional and spiritual. He was given a glimpse of what might have been, what could have been for him.

Will that be your experience? Will you look from hell into heaven and lament over all the gospel sermons you heard and rejected? Will you regret so glibly dismissing the truth of the love of God which alone could have got you into heaven? Will you remember a time when perhaps God spoke to your heart and conscience and showed you your sin, but you refused to listen?

No hope in hell

Why should Jesus tell us such a terrible story? It must be in order to warn us of the reality of that which so many easily dismiss. Obviously Jesus took no pleasure in picturing this soul in hell, but he was showing us that there is no hope in hell. The words of the rich man are full of anguish: 'Have pity on me and send Lazarus to dip the tip of his finger in water and cool my tongue, because I am in agony in this fire.'

But nothing can be done for a soul in hell. Not even God, not even the blood of Christ, can do anything, because hell is final. There is no second chance. There is no gospel preaching in hell, no opportunities to join in worship, no prayers offered by others on your behalf. There are no hymns, no sacraments; there is no hope in hell — only torment and anguish. There is no bridge from hell to heaven. There is a great chasm that has been fixed and no one can cross (Luke 16:26).

Hope in Christ

There is no bridge from hell to heaven, but there is a bridge from sin to God. The chasm that separates a sinner from God is enormous, but the grace and mercy and love of God in Christ have spanned it. For centuries men have tried to build bridges of religion and morality from their depraved condition into the presence of the holy God. They all fall short, but God himself has built a bridge, not from hell to heaven but from sin to God. Christ himself is that bridge because he dealt with our sin, took its condemnation and guilt and faced the wrath of God instead of us. Salvation is when a sinner is lifted by the grace of God out of his sin and placed in a new and living relationship with God for all eternity. It is the Lord Jesus Christ alone who can do this. There is hope in Christ, but there is no hope after death.

Questions for personal thought or group discussion

1. Why is nominal religion no answer to death and hell?
2. How can the existence of hell be compatible with the belief in a God of love?
3. Is there any escape from hell?
4. In what way does Christ offer sinners hope of escaping hell?

15.

Listen to God

Luke 16:19-31; 24:13-35

The parable concludes with a dialogue between the rich man and Abraham concerning the five living brothers of the man in hell. The rich man was anxious that his brothers should not also go to hell and asked that Lazarus should be sent to warn them. Neither he nor his brothers would have paid the slightest attention to Lazarus the beggar, but Lazarus the dead man come back from the grave would be something else. That was the rich man's thinking. He believed that no one could ignore the testimony of someone who had come back from the dead.

Abraham, however, disagreed with him and argued that all the five brothers needed to do to escape hell was to listen to and believe what God says in the Scriptures.

Here we have more than the opinion of two men; they represent the two great philosophies, or attitudes, concerning the way in which a person will come to faith. The popular attitude is that 'Seeing is believing'. Let an unbeliever see a miracle and he will believe. The other view, represented here by Abraham, is that faith comes by hearing the Word of God. This is God's way of salvation, and therefore it should be enough for any unbeliever. He or she needs to listen, not see.

The popular view

It is not difficult to sympathize with the rich man's way of thinking. It seems so obvious and it comes from a man who had a genuine concern for the welfare of others. In hell he came to realize that unless something was done about it, his five brothers were going to join him in that terrible place. How did he know that? What right did he have to sit in judgement upon his brothers? This man knew his brothers. He knew that, when it came down to it, they were no different from him and their lives were marked by godlessness and sin.

The five brothers may well have been different in temperament and outlook from each other. One may have been a good husband, or another kind to animals. There may have been a loud-mouthed fool among them, or a drunkard, or a thief. But these ultimately are not the issues that determine where a man spends eternity. The rich man, knowing his brothers well and knowing their different peculiarities, believed they were all going to hell. But the brothers themselves would not have believed that. They would never have thought of going to hell; no one does. Most people don't believe in hell, and even those who do will rarely imagine that they themselves are going there.

The rich man knew by terrible experience of the reality of hell. He knew why he was there and he believed his brothers would join him. It is quite remarkable that a soul in hell should want to save others from going there, but that is the parable. He could see only one way to prevent his brothers from joining him, and that was to show them a miracle and prove beyond doubt to them that there is life after death.

The rich man in hell could think of no other way. God, grace and mercy still had no place in his thinking. He was as wrong in hell as he had been during his lifetime on earth. His concern for his brothers was commendable, but his thinking still totally disregarded God. Even hell had not mellowed his attitude towards the Lord of glory.

Abraham did not believe that the rich man's answer would work, and he was right. Someone called Lazarus had already come back from the dead. He was a different Lazarus, but he had been dead and buried for four days and everybody knew it. Probably most of the people in the village of Bethany had gone to his funeral and seen him put in the tomb, but four days later they saw him walking the streets of Bethany once again. He had been raised from the dead by the power of the Lord Jesus Christ. No one could doubt the fact of this, but still people did not believe in Jesus. Some of them treated Lazarus as something of a circus freak. They followed Jesus, not because they now recognized who he was, but to see this Lazarus who had been dead and whom Jesus had raised from the dead. They saw the miracle, but it created no faith in God in their hearts.

When Jesus was hanging on the cross the bystanders mocked him and goaded him with the challenge that if he came down from the cross they would believe in him. But when he rose from the dead on Easter morning they still did not believe. With all the evidence of the resurrection, they still did not want to believe.

People talk about blind faith, but there are few things so blind as stubborn unbelief. In his book, *Does God believe in Atheists?* John Blanchard makes the same point in regard to men's belief in evolution: 'Writing in *Nature* as long ago as 1929, biologist D. M. S. Watson brazenly conceded, "The theory of evolution itself [is] a theory universally accepted, *not because it can be proved by logically coherent evidence to be true*, but because the only alternative is special creation, which is clearly incredible" (emphasis added).'[1] Blanchard then goes on to quote the eminent British anthropologist Sir Arthur Keith: 'Evolution is *unproved and unprovable*. We believe it only because the alternative is special creation, which is unthinkable (emphasis added).'[2]

Men will believe anything rather than believe in God. To them belief in God is incredible and unthinkable.

Listen to God

Abraham's advice to the rich man is both simple and devastating: Listen to God or you are left with no hope. This is not over-simplifying a serious problem. It is the only answer that works. God speaks through his Word. The term 'Moses and the Prophets' is a reference to the Old Testament. Today we have not only Moses and the Prophets, but also the apostles. We have the whole of God's revealed truth in the Bible.

The basic and foundational message of the Bible, whether in the writings of Moses or the New Testament, is atonement and substitution. This is why Jesus was able to teach the two disciples on the road to Emmaus about his own ministry using the Old Testament: 'Beginning with Moses and all the Prophets, he explained to them what was said in all the Scriptures concerning himself' (Luke 24:27). In the Gospels Jesus quoted from over thirty different Old Testament passages to help make his message clear. In Luke 4 alone, we find the Saviour quoting three verses from Deuteronomy to expose the lies of Satan and then, after reading aloud Isaiah 61:1-2, he declared, 'Today this scripture is fulfilled in your hearing.'

Jesus was able to use the Old Testament in this way because it speaks of him from Genesis to Malachi. The message of atonement and substitution is illustrated on numerous occasions in the Old Testament and then brought to its glorious reality in the death of Jesus on the cross. So the writer to the Hebrews is able to refer back to the Old Testament tabernacle and its sacrifices and say, 'When Christ came as high priest of the good things that are already here, he went through the greater and more perfect tabernacle that is not man-made, that is to say, not a part of this creation. He did not enter by means of the blood of goats and calves; but he entered the Most Holy Place once for all by his own blood, having obtained eternal redemption. The blood of goats and bulls and the ashes of a heifer sprinkled on those who are ceremonially unclean sanctify them so that they are outwardly clean. How much more, then, will the blood of Christ, who through the eternal Spirit offered himself unblemished to God, cleanse our consciences from acts that lead to death, so that we may serve the living God!' (Hebrews 9:11-15).

'Pay attention to the Scriptures; listen to what God says,' was Abraham's response to the rich man's request. It would have been enough to save his five brothers from hell, and it is enough to save anyone, if we believe and act upon what we read in the Bible. The Scripture says, 'But now a righteousness from God, apart from law, has been made known, to which the Law and the Prophets testify. This righteousness from God comes through faith in Jesus Christ to all who believe' (Rom. 3:21-22).

None of us is fit for heaven and we all deserve hell. To escape hell we need a righteousness that is acceptable to God. What we need, God graciously provides for us. This righteousness that God gives us can never be earned; we can never deserve it, and there is nothing we can do in order to qualify for it. In the next chapter in Romans Paul refers to Abraham. He is talking about salvation and asks what Abraham did to gain this blessing of God: 'What then shall we say that Abraham, our forefather, discovered in this matter? If, in fact, Abraham was justified by works, he had something to boast about — but not before God. What does the Scripture say? "Abraham believed God, and it was credited to him as righteousness"' (Romans 4:1-3). Abraham believed the Scriptures. He listened to what God said and trusted in what God did, and this was the means of his salvation. Abraham's salvation, and ours, depends upon the grace of God in what Jesus Christ did for us. We need to listen to the message of the gospel.

Questions for personal thought or group discussion

1. Is it true that 'Seeing is believing'?
2. Discuss the two quotations from John Blanchard.
3. Why is it so important to listen to God?
4. Are the Scriptures the only reliable guide to what God wants us to know?

Conclusion: the gospel

The gospel is the good news of what God has done for guilty sinners in and through the Lord Jesus Christ.

The word 'gospel' means 'good news', and the gospel message is good news in contrast to the awful predicament that all men and women are in because of their sin. Sin is the breaking of the law of God, and we are all guilty of it. It is not something which holds people against their will, but Jesus said, 'Men loved darkness instead of light because their deeds were evil' (John 3:19). This sin puts us under the wrath of God. Make no mistake about it: God will not tolerate sin.

Clearly the fact that we are under condemnation is not good news, but it is crucial that sinners understand and believe this if they are to benefit from God's good news in the gospel.

Good news

The good news is that 'God so loved the world that he gave his only begotten Son, that whoever believes in him shall not perish but have eternal life' (John 3:16). This divine love was not mere pity, but actually did something about man's terrible condition. God gave his Son to take our guilt and punishment upon himself and die in the place of sinners. The gospel is the message which explains all that is involved in God's work of saving sinners.

It is the gospel of God (Romans 1:1) and describes, not what we can achieve if only we will try harder, but what God alone has done for us. It originates in the heart of God himself and is the record of what the love and grace of God have done for guilty sinners. It tells us of the uniqueness of Jesus. He alone is the Saviour whom the gospel reveals.

Who is Jesus?

The first chapter of the New Testament introduces the Saviour to us and Matthew uses two names for him, Jesus and Immanuel.

- *Jesus* means 'Saviour' and tells us what he came into the world to do.
- *Immanuel* means 'God with us' and tells us that he was no ordinary person. Jesus is God.

The good news is that when Jesus died on the cross he did so in the place of guilty sinners to save them from God's anger against sin and the judgement they deserve. He alone was innocent of sin, and was the only one who could act as our substitute. He stood in the place of his people whom he came to save and bore for us the punishment we deserved.

The cross was God's supreme act of love and grace.

- At the cross we see God, in all his divine holiness, dealing with human sin.
- At the cross God removed the barrier of sin that separates us from him by making his Son, the Lord Jesus Christ, responsible for our violations of divine law, and exacting from him the full punishment that was due to us.
- At the cross God credits our sin and guilt to Jesus and at the same time credits Jesus' righteousness to us.
- At the cross God's wrath fell upon his Son instead of us.

Sin is punished, as God prescribed it should be. This is the gospel.

The demands of the gospel

The gospel demands the same sort of commitment from its recipients as it had from its author. Jesus gave all he was and had to bring the gospel into being. His obedience to the heavenly Father's will was absolute and total. Therefore, the gospel has no sympathy with nominal, half-hearted, insipid Christianity.

It says to the person whose Christianity consists merely of church attendance and vague religious observances, 'Your religion is an insult to the message and purpose of Jesus Christ. You need to take God seriously and believe the entire gospel. If you do not you will forever go on living a life that seeks to fool God with outward rites but has no inward experience of grace, love and mercy.'

It says to the genuine, born-again Christian who has let his spiritual life become loose and flabby, 'Get some direction into your life; get some commitment instead of compromise into your Christian experience. In the light of what Jesus Christ has done for you, a life that is a living sacrifice to God is both reasonable and necessary.'

It may be that, like Ananias, you want a reputation among Christians but are not prepared to earn it. It may be that, like David, you are in the wrong place and in the wrong frame of mind. If so, there is only one remedy. Come back again to the gospel message of the love and grace of God in Christ. View again Jesus dying in your place on the cross and determine to live only for his glory. Stop playing around with Christianity and submerge yourself in all that God has for you in Christ.

Notes

Chapter 5 — You can wash your hands but the guilt remains
1. C. H. Spurgeon, *The Gospel of the Kingdom,* Marshall, 1893, p.246.

Chapter 6 — The kiss of a friend
1. John Brown, *Discourses and Sayings of our Lord,* Banner of Truth, 1967, vol. 2, p.433.
2. J. C. Ryle, *Expository Thoughts on John,* James Clark, vol. 3, pp.213-14.
3. Brown, *Discourses and Sayings,* p.431.
4. J. M. MacArthur, *MacArthur New Testament Commentary* (CD-ROM), Parsons Technology.

Chapter 10 — The sin of a good man
1. A. W. Pink, *The Life of David,* Baker Book House, 1985, p.17.
2. Roger Ellsworth, *The Shepherd King,* Evangelical Press, 1998, pp.206-7.

Chapter 12 — 'I don't believe that'
1. L. Boettner, *Immortality,* P & R, 1973, p.59.

Chapter 13 — Death and hell
1. Boettner, *Immortality,* p.16.
2. As above, p.18.

Chapter 15 — Listen to God
1. John Blanchard, *Does God Believe in Atheists?*, Evangelical Press,
2000, p.109.
2. As above, p.110.

A wide range of excellent books on spiritual subjects is available from Evangelical Press. Please write to us for your free catalogue or contact us by e-mail.

Evangelical Press
Faverdale North Industrial Estate, Darlington, DL3 0PH, England

Evangelical Press USA
P. O. Box 84, Auburn, MA 01501, USA

e-mail: sales@evangelicalpress.org

web: http://www.evangelicalpress.org